FLEMISH PAINTERS
VOLUME TWO

Frontispiece. London Virgin with a Firescreen Painter: *The Virgin and Child*. London N.G.

FLEMISH PAINTERS

1430-1830

by

R. H. WILENSKI

VOLUME TWO

A Reynal Book

THE VIKING PRESS

NEW YORK

Printed in Great Britain

CONTENTS

NOTE TO THE GENERAL READER

The arrangement of the plates is basically chronological (though I have occasionally placed a picture out of its position to point a comparison or contrast).

The successive changes in pictorial style and the overlapping of styles are thus made evident.

The letter *s.* in brackets after the title of a picture in a caption stands for 'signed'; *m.* stands for monogrammed; *doc.* stands for documented.

Unless the word 'Detail' is included in the caption the whole picture is reproduced. Exceptions are Plates 872 and 873 which are a little trimmed at the top and Plate 883 which is a little trimmed on the right hand side.

The INDEX OF PAINTERS (pp. xv–xvii in this volume) gives the plate numbers of the works reproduced by each artist.

Mentions of these painters in the general conspectus contained in PART I of VOLUME I can be found by reference to the INDEX TO PART I in that volume.

Further information about the painters can be found in the DICTIONARY OF FLEMISH PAINTERS which constitutes PART II of VOLUME I and is alphabetically arranged.

NOTE TO SPECIALIST STUDENTS

When a date is included in my captions to the plates it is always either on the picture or known by documentation; it is never a conjecture on style grounds.

As explained in my NOTE TO SPECIALIST STUDENTS in VOLUME I, when a conventional name of my invention (ending with the word 'Painter') is used for the painter of a picture of unknown authorship, e.g. **London Virgin with a Firescreen Painter** (Frontispiece), the authorship presumed by the compiler of the museum catalogue at the time of writing can be found in the entry for my invented name in the DICTIONARY OF FLEMISH PAINTERS which constitutes PART II of VOLUME I.

ACKNOWLEDGEMENTS

Pictures in the English Royal Collection are reproduced by gracious permission of Her Majesty the Queen.

American and other museums were most courteously cooperative when my publishers were collecting the hundreds of photographs which I asked for and from which my selections for the reproductions in this volume were eventually made.

INDEX OF OWNERS

N.B. The figures indicate the numbers of the plates in this volume.

INDEX OF OWNERS

INDEX OF PAINTERS

N.B. The figures indicate the numbers of the plates in this volume.

INDEX OF PAINTERS

INDEX OF PAINTERS

REPRODUCTIONS
OF PAINTINGS

PLATE 1

Pl. 1. New York Crucifixion and Last Judgement Painter: *Detail of Pl. 3*

PLATE 2

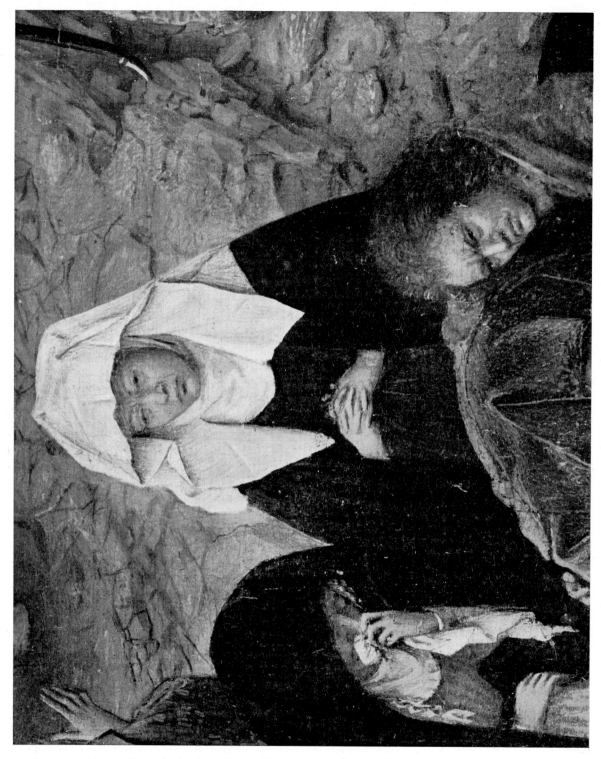

Pl. 2. New York Crucifixion and Last Judgement Painter: *Detail of Pl. 3*

New York Crucifixion and Last Judgement Painter

Pl. 3. *The Crucifixion*. New York Met.   Pl. 4. *The Last Judgement*. New York Met.

PLATE 5

Pl. 5. New York Crucifixion and Last Judgement Painter: *Detail of Pl. 3*

PLATE 6

Pl. 6. New York Crucifixion and Last Judgement Painter: *Detail of Pl. 3*

PLATE 7

Pl. 7. New York Crucifixion and Last Judgement Painter: *Detail of Pl. 4*

PLATE 8

Pl. 8. New York Crucifixion and Last Judgement Painter: *Detail of Pl. 4*

PLATE 9

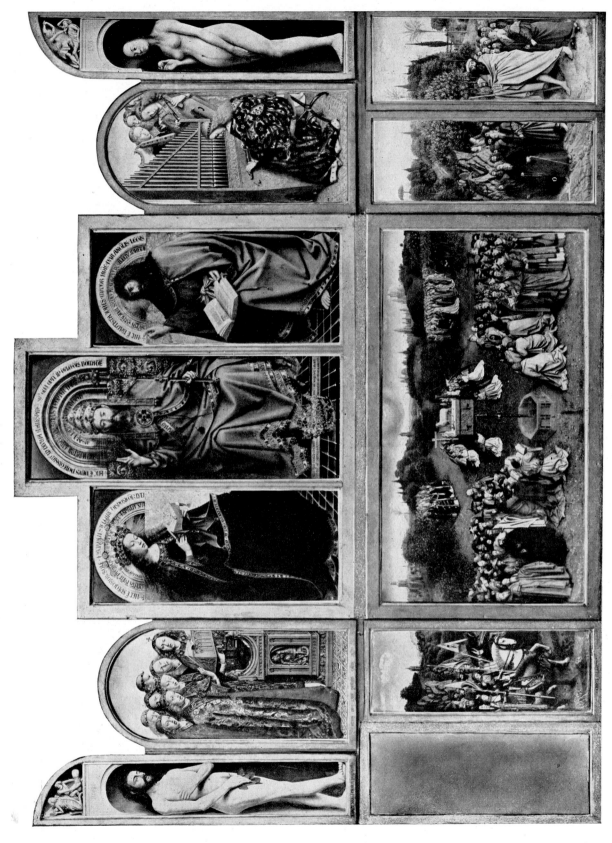

Pl. 9. Hubert and Jan van Eyck: *The Altarpiece of the Mystic Lamb (inscribed and 1432).* Ghent S. Bavon

PLATE 10

Pl. 10. J. van Eyck: *A young man* (*Timotheos*) (*s* and 1432). London N.G.

PLATE 11

Pl. 11. Hubert and Jan van Eyck: *Jodoc Vyt, donor* (detail of Pl. 12)

PLATE 12

Pl. 12. Hubert and Jan van Eyck: *The Altarpiece of the Mystic Lamb* (closed). Ghent S. Bavon

PLATE 13

Pl. 13. Hubert and Jan van Eyck: *The Virgin* (detail of Pl. 9)

Pl. 14. J. van der Veken: Copy of panel stolen (1934) from the *Altarpiece of the Mystic Lamb* (detail of Pl. 9). Ghent S. Bavon

Pl. 15. Washington Annunciation in a Church Painter: *The Annunciation*. Washington N.G.

PLATE 16

Pl. 16. New York Crucifixion and Last Judgement Painter: *Detail of Pl. 4*

PLATE 17

Pl. 17. Hubert and Jan van Eyck: *Singing Angels* (detail of Pl. 9)

PLATE 18

Pl. 18. J. van Eyck: *S. Barbara* (*s* and 1437). Antwerp

Pl. 18A. J. van Eyck: *The Marriage of Giovanni Arnolfini and Giovanna Cenami* (s and 1434). London N.G.

Pl. 19. J. van Eyck: *The Virgin and Child with SS. Donatian and George and the Donor, Canon van der Paele.*
(*Van der Paele altarpiece*) (*s* and 1436). Bruges

Pl. 20. J. van Eyck: *Margaret, wife of the painter* (*s* and 1439).
Bruges

Pl. 21. J. van Eyck: *Man in a red turban* (*s* and 1433).
London N.G.

PLATE 22

Pl. 22. Madrid Fountain of Grace Painter: *The Fountain of Grace*. Madrid

PLATE 23

Pl. 23. Hubert and Jan van Eyck: *Detail of Pl. 9*

Pl. 25. J. van Eyck: *Virgin and Child by a fountain* (s and 1439) Antwerp

Pl. 24. New York Virgin in a Tabernacle Painter: *Virgin and Child.* New York Met.

PLATE 26

Pl. 26. New York Annunciation in a Porch Painter: *The Annunciation*. New York Met.

Pl. 27. P. Christus: *The Virgin and Child with SS. Jerome and Francis* (*s* and 14.7). Frankfort Staedel

Pl. 28. Minneapolis Adoration Painter: *Detail of Pl. 75*   Pl. 29. Minneapolis Adoration Painter: *Detail of Pl. 75*

PLATE 30

Pl. 30. Washington Nativity in a Sculptured Porch Painter: *The Nativity*. Washington N.G.

PLATE 31

Pl. 31. P. Christus: *Portrait of a Carthusian* (s and 1446). New York Met.

Pl. 32. London Christ appearing to his Mother Painter:
Christ appearing to his Mother. London N.G.

Pl. 33. New York Christ appearing to his Mother Painter:
Detail of Pl. 47

Pl. 34. Beaune Last Judgement
Painter: Detail of *Last Judgement*. Beaune Hospices

Pl. 35. Flémalle Master: *S. Veronica*. Frankfort Staedel.

Pl. 36. Flémalle Master: *The Virgin and Child*. Frankfort Staedel.

Pl. 37. Flémalle Master: *The Trinity*. Frankfort Staedel.

Pl. 38. Cambridge Veronica Draughtsman: *S. Veronica*.
Cambridge Fitz.

PLATE 39

Pl. 39. London Virgin with a Firescreen Painter: *Detail of frontispiece*

PLATE 40

Pl. 40. London Woman in a Wimple Painter: *Portrait of a woman*. London N.G.

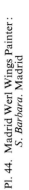

Pl. 44. Madrid Werl Wings Painter:
S. Barbara. Madrid

Pl. 42. Beaune Last Judgement Painter:
Detail of *Last Judgement.* Beaune Hospices

Pl. 43. London Magdalene reading Painter:

Pl. 41. Madrid Werl Wings Painter:
*Donor Henricus Werl with S. John the
Baptist* (1438). Madrid

PLATE 45

Pl. 45. Antwerp Philippe de Croy Painter: *Philippe de Croy, Seigneur de Sempy as an adorant.* Antwerp

PLATE 46

Pl 46 R van der Weyden · *Descent from the Cross (doc.)*. Madrid

Pl. 48. Boston S. Luke Painter: *S. Luke drawing the Virgin.*
Boston

Pl. 47. New York Christ appearing to His Mother Painter:
Christ appearing to His Mother. New York Met.

PLATE 49

Pl. 49. Boston S. Luke Painter: *Detail of Pl. 48*

PLATE 50

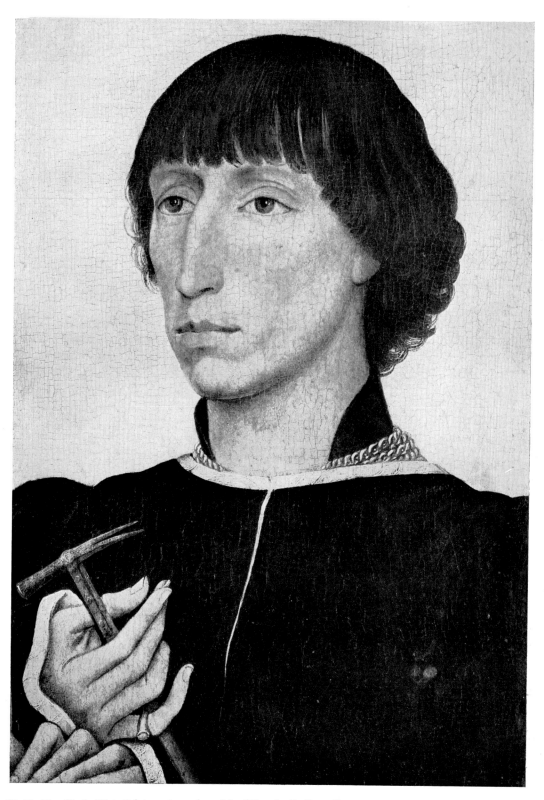

Pl. 50. New York d'Este Painter: *A member of the d'Este family (Leonello, Francesco or Meliaduse)*. New York Met.

PLATE 51

Pl. 51. Redemption Master: *Crucifixion in a church*. Madrid

Pl. 52. Redemption Master:
Expulsion from Eden (wing of Pl. 51). Madrid

Pl. 53. Redemption Master:
The Last Judgement (wing of Pl. 51). Madrid

Pl. 54. Exhumation of S. Hubert Master: *The Exhumation of S. Hubert A.D. 825*. London N.G.

Pl. 55. Detroit S. Jerome Painter:
S. Jerome in his study (detail). Detroit

Pl. 56. London S. Giles Mass Painter:
Detail of Pl. 83

PLATE 57

Pl. 57. London Young Woman in White Head-dress Painter: *Portrait of a young woman*. London N.G.

PLATE 58

Pl. 58. D. Bouts: *Last Supper* (*doc*. 1464–1467). Louvain S. Pierre

PLATE 59

Pl. 59. Young Man in High Cap Painter: *Portrait of a young man* (1462). London N.G.

PLATE 60

Pl. 60. New York Man in High Cap Painter: *Head of an adorant*. New York Met.

PLATE 61

Pl. 61. D. Bouts: *The meeting of Abraham and Melchizedek (doc.)* (wing of Pl. 58). Louvain S. Pierre

PLATE 62

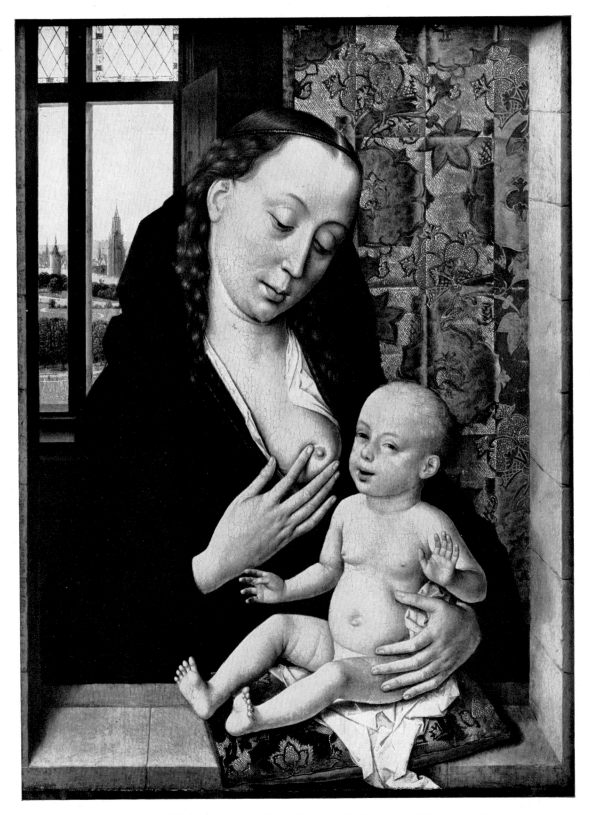

Pl. 62. London Virgin with Brocade Screen Painter: *The Virgin and Child*. London N.G.

PLATE 63

Pl. 63. Lille Path to Paradise Painter: *The Path to Paradise*. Lille

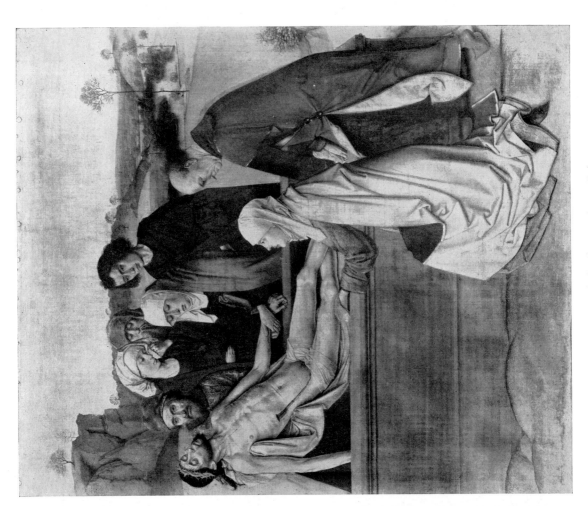

PLATE 66

Pl. 66. Vienna Adam and Eve Painter: *The Fall*. Vienna Kunsthist.

PLATE 67

Pl. 67. D. Bouts: *The Unjust Judgement of Emperor Otho* (*doc.*). Brussels

PLATE 68

Pl. 68. Washington Man with an Arrow Painter. *Young man with an arrow*. Washington N.G.

PLATE 69

Pl. 69. D. Bouts.: *The Ordeal by Fire* (*doc.*). Brussels

PLATE 70

Pl. 70. Hugo of Antwerp: *Detail of Pl. 78*

Pl. 71. New York Lady with a Pink Painter:
Lady in a hennin with a pink. New York Met.

Pl. 72. Ursula Legend Master: *S. Ursula leaving Rome* (detail). Bruges Couvent des Sœurs Noires

Pl. 73. Ursula Legend Master: *Detail of Pl. 99*

Pl. 74. Ursula Legend Master: *Detail of Pl. 101*

PLATE 75

Pl. 75. Minneapolis Adoration Painter: *Adoration of the Shepherds*. Minneapolis

PLATE 76

Pl. 76. Hugo of Antwerp: *The Portinari Altarpiece (doc.), Adoration of the Shepherds.* Florence Uffizi

Pl. 78. Hugo of Antwerp: *SS. Margaret and Mary Magdalene with Portinari's wife and daughter* (wing of Pl. 76). Florence Uffizi

Pl. 77. Hugo of Antwerp: *SS. Thomas and Anthony Abbot with donor Tommaso Portinari and two sons* (wing of Pl. 76). Florence Uffizi

Pl. 80. Hugo of Antwerp: *Detail of Pl. 78*

Pl. 79. Hugo of Antwerp: *Detail of Pl. 77*

PLATE 81

Pl. 81. Hugo of Antwerp: *Detail of Pl. 78*

Pl. 84. H. Memlinc: *Presentation in the Temple* (wing of Pl. 85). Bruges Hôpital S. Jean

Pl. 83. London S. Giles Mass Painter: *Mass of S. Giles* (*shown in Paris S. Denis*). London N.G.

Pl. 82. H. Memlinc: *The Nativity* (wing of Pl. 85). Bruges Hôpital S. Jean

PLATE 85

Pl. 85. H. Memlinc: *The Floreins Altar (inscribed and 1479). Adoration of the Magi.* Bruges Hôpital S. Jean

Pl. 86. Pearl of Brabant Master: *Adoration of the Magi*. Munich

Pl. 87. Tiburtine Sibyl Master: *The Virgin appearing to the Tiburtine Sibyl and the Emperor Augustus*
Frankfort Staedel

Pl. 88. H. Memlinc: *Detail of Pl. 90*

Pl. 89. H. Memlinc: *Beheading of S. John the Baptist*
(wing of Pl. 111). Bruges Hôpital S. Jean

Pl. 90. H. Memlinc: *S. John on Patmos* (wing of Pl. 111).
Bruges Hôpital S. Jean

Pl. 91. Pearl of Brabant Master:
S. John the Baptist (wing of Pl. 86). Munich

Pl. 92. Pearl of Brabant Master:
S. Christopher (wing of Pl. 86). Munich

Pl. 93. H. Memlinc: *The S. Ursula Shrine; Scenes from the Legend of S. Ursula* (*doc.*). Bruges Hôpital S. Jean

94. H. Memlinc: *S. John the Baptist* (wing, exterior, of Pl. 85)   Pl. 95. H. Memlinc: *S. Veronica* (wing, exterior, of Pl. 85)

PLATE 96

Pl. 96. New York Crucifixion and Last Judgement Painter: *S. Michael* (detail of Pl. 4)

Pl 96A. Bruges Virgin with the Apple Painter: *The Virgin and Child (with Niewnenhove arms)* (1487). Bruges. Hôpital Saint-Jean

Ursula Legend Master

Pl. 97. *Arrival of S. Ursula at Cologne*　　　　　　Pl. 98. *Arrival of S. Ursula at Tiel*

Pl. 99. *Departure of S. Ursula from Bâle*　　　Pl. 100. *Martyrdom of S. Ursula, her companions and Pope Cyriacus*

Bruges Couvent des Sœurs Noires

Pl. 103. Ursula Legend Master:
Veneration of the relics of S. Ursula.
Bruges Couvent des Sœurs Noires

Pl. 102. Dublin S. Augustine Painter:
Scenes from the life of S. Augustine.
Dublin N.G.I.

Pl. 101. Ursula Legend Master:
The envoy of King Agrippinus.
Bruges Couvent des Sœurs Noires

PLATE 104

Pl. 104. Philadelphia Adorant Painter: *Young man in prayer*. Philadelphia

PLATE 105

Pl. 105. London (Layard) Virgin and Child Painter: *The Virgin and Child*. London N.G.

PLATE 106

Pl. 106. Buckingham Palace Mystic Marriage Painter: *Mystic marriage of S. Catherine*. London H.M. the Queen

Pl. 107. Brussels Mystic Marriage Painter: *Mystic marriage of S. Catherine*. Brussels

Pl. 108. Philadelphia S. Catherine Painter:
S. Catherine. Philadelphia

Pl. 109. New York S. Catherine Painter: *S. Catherine*.
New York Met.

PLATE 110

Pl. 110. Detroit Mystic Marriage Painter: *Mystic marriage of S. Catherine*. Detroit

Pl. 111. H. Memlinc: *S. John Altar. Mystic marriage of S. Catherine with SS. Barbara, John the Baptist and John the Evangelist* (*inscribed* and 1479). Bruges Hôpital S. Jean

Pl. 112. H. Memlinc: *The S. Ursula shrine. Scenes from the Legend of S. Ursula.* (*doc.*) Bruges Hôpital S. Jean

Pl. 113. H. Memlinc: *Detail of Pl. 89*

Pl. 114. H. Memlinc: *SS. James the Great and Anthony with donors* (wing, exterior, of Pl. 111)

Pl. 115. H. Memlinc: *SS. Agnes and Claire with women donors* (wing, exterior, of Pl. 111)

Lucy Legend Master: *Scenes from the Life of S. Lucy* (1480). Bruges S. Jacques

Pl. 116. *S. Lucy denounced as a Christian before the Consul*

Pl. 117. *S. Lucy and her mother*

Pl. 118. *Oxen failing to drag S. Lucy to a brothel*

Pl. 119. Tiburtine Sibyl Master: *Detail of Pl. 87*

Pl. 120. Ursula Legend Master: *Detail of Pl. 103*

Pl. 121. Minneapolis S. Catherine Painter: *S. Catherine*.
Minneapolis

Pl. 123. Dublin S. Nicholas Painter: *Two miracles of S. Nicholas of Bari*. Dublin N.G.I.

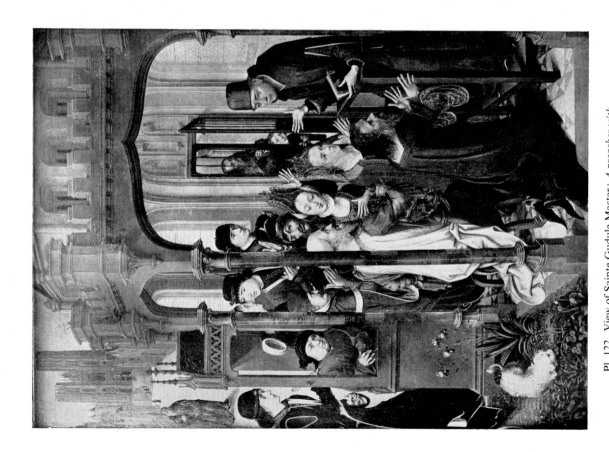

Pl. 122. View of Sainte Gudule Master: *A preacher with Brussels Sainte Gudule in background*. Paris Louvre

PLATE 124

Pl. 124. Geertgen tot Sint Jans: *Julian the Apostate burning the bones of S. John the Baptist and members of the Order of S. John with some rescued bones* (*doc.*). Vienna Kunsthist.

Pl. 126. Liverpool Entombment Painter: *The Entombment.*
Liverpool Walker

Pl. 125. New York Lamentation Painter: *Lamentation.*
New York Met.

PLATE 127

Pl. 127. Geertgen tot Sint Jans: *Lamentation* (*doc.*). Vienna Kunsthist.

PLATE 128

Pl. 128. Virgo inter Virgines Master: *The Virgin and Child with SS. Catherine and Ursula, Barbara and Cecilia.*
Amsterdam Rijks.

PLATE 129

Pl. 129. London Nativity by Night Painter: *The Nativity*. London N.G.

PLATE 130

Pl. 130. St. Louis Entombment Painter: *The Entombment*. St. Louis

PLATE 131

Pl. 131. Philadelphia Maria Egyptiaca Painter: *S. Mary of Egypt penitent in the desert*. Philadelphia

PLATE 132

Pl. 132. Philadelphia S. Christopher Painter: *S. Christopher*. Philadelphia

PLATE 133

Pl. 133. Florence (Poggio Imperiale) Crucifixion Painter: *The Crucifixion*. Florence Uffizi

PLATE 134

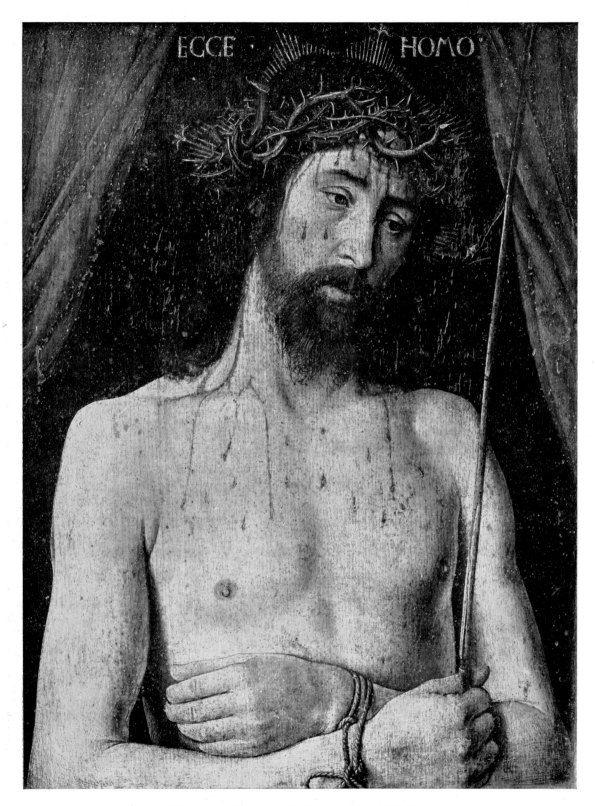

Pl. 134. J. Hey: *Christ crowned with thorns* (*s* and 1494). Brussels

Pl. 135. Antwerp Last Judgement Painter: *Last Judgement with Seven Works of Mercy and Seven Deadly Sins.* Antwerp

Beaune Last Judgement Painter: Details of *Last Judgement.* Beaune Hospices

Pl. 136. *Cross and Crown of Thorns*   Pl. 137. *Saints and the Blessed*   Pl. 138. *Saints and the Damned*   Pl. 139. *Lance, sponge and column*

PLATE 140

Pl. 140. New York Godelieve Legend Painter: *Marriage of S. Godelieve* (detail of Pl. 141)

New York Godelieve Legend Painter: *Scenes from the legend of S. Godelieve of Ghistelles.* New York Met.

Pl. 141. *Central panel of polyptych*

Pls. 142, 143, 144, 145. *Wings of polyptych*

PLATE 146

Pl. 146. Malines Guild of S. George Master: *S. George with two Bishops and Members of the Malines Crossbowmen's Guild.*
Antwerp

PLATE 147

Pl. 147. Toledo Marriage of Henry VI Painter: *Marriage of Henry VI with Margaret of Anjou*. Toledo (U.S.A.)

PLATE 148

Pl. 148. Melbourne Miracles Painter: *Miracle of the loaves and fishes*. Melbourne, Victoria N.G.

Pl. 149. Melbourne Miracles Painter: *Marriage at Cana* (wing of Pl. 148). Melbourne Victoria N.G.

Pl. 150. Melbourne Miracles Painter: *The Raising of Lazarus* (wing of Pl. 148). Melbourne Victoria N.G.

PLATE 151

Pl. 151. New York Adoration in a White Castle Painter: *Adoration of the Magi*. New York Met.

PLATE 152

Pl. 152. Philadelphia Marriage of the Virgin Painter: *Scenes from the life of the Virgin*. Philadelphia

Pl. 154. Glasgow Saint and Donor Painter: *Saint and Donor*.
Glasgow

Pl. 153. Worcester Saint and Donor Painter: *Saint and donor*.
Worcester, U.S.A.

PLATE 155

Pl. 155. Giles Master: *S. Giles and the hind.* London N.G.

PLATE 156

Pl. 156. H. Bosch: *Mass of S. Gregory* (*s*) (wings closed on Pl. 157). Madrid

PLATE 157

Pl. 157. H. Bosch: *Adoration of the Magi* (*s*) (centre of triptych). Madrid

PLATE 158

Pl. 158. H. Bosch: *Detail of Pl. 156*

PLATE 159

Pl. 159. New York Crucifixion and Last Judgement Painter: *Detail of Pl. 1*

PLATE 160

Pl. 160. New York Crucifixion and Last Judgement Painter: *Detail of Pl. 3*

PLATE 161

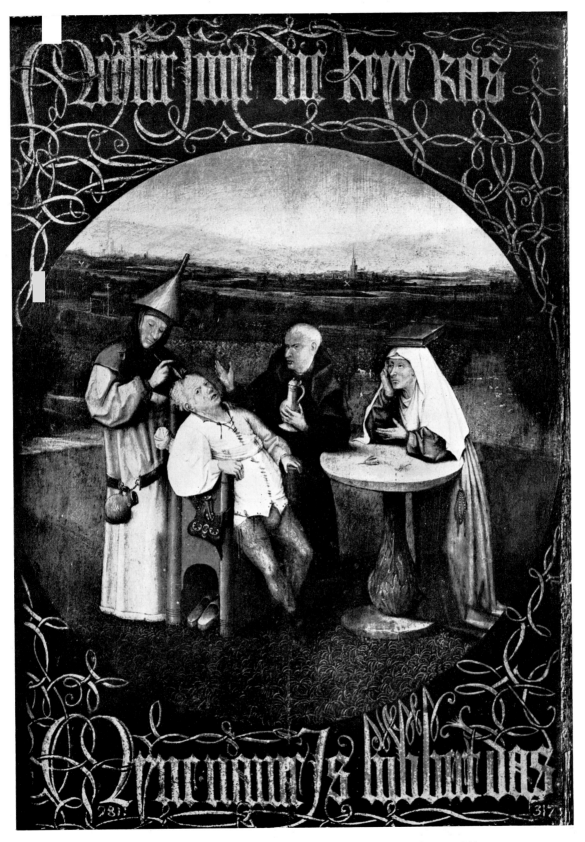

Pl. 161. H. Bosch: *The Operation for Stone: or the Cure of Folly* (*doc.*). Madrid

PLATE 162

Pl. 162. Philadelphia Adoration of Magi Painter: *Adoration of the Magi*. Philadelphia

PLATE 163

Pl. 163. H. Bosch: *Temptation of S. Anthony* (*doc.*). Madrid

PLATE 164

Pl. 164. H. Bosch: *Christ driving the moneychangers from the Temple* (s). Glasgow

Pl. 164A. H. Bosch: *The Garden of Eden (Detail of left wing of Haywain triptych)*. Madrid

PLATE 165

Pl. 165. H. Bosch: *The Haywain* (s) (centre of triptych). Madrid

PLATE 166

Pl. 166. H. Bosch: *The Garden of Delights* (*The Millennium?*) (*doc.*) (centre of triptych). Madrid

Pl. 166A. H. Bosch: *Devils building a tower in Hell* (*Detail of right wing of Haywain triptych*).
Madrid

167. H. Bosch: *The Creation of Eve* (wing of Pl. 166). Madrid

Pl. 168. H. Bosch: *Hell* (wing of Pl. 166). Madrid

PLATE 169

Pl. 169. H. Bosch: *Detail of Pl. 166*

PLATE 170

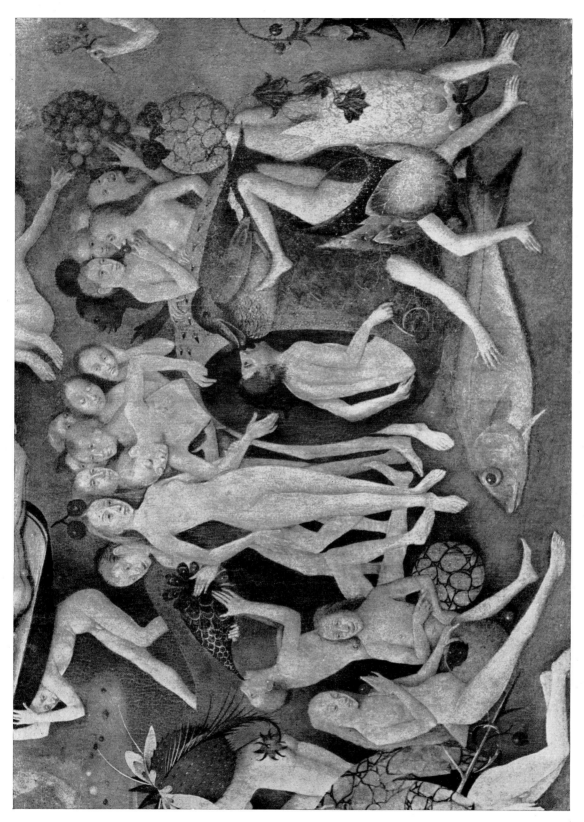

Pl. 170. H. Bosch: *Detail of Pl. 166*

PLATE 171

Pl. 171. H. Bosch: *Detail of Pl. 166*

Pl. 172. H. Bosch: *Creation of the World* (wings closed on triptych, Pls. 166, 167, 168). Madrid

Pl. 173. H. Bosch: *Detail of Pl. 168*

PLATE 174

Pl. 174. Princeton Christ before Pilate Painter: *Christ before Pilate*. Princeton University

PLATE 175

Pl. 175. London Christ Mocked Painter: *The Crowning with Thorns*. London N.G.

PLATE 176

Pl. 176. Oultremont Master: *Descent from the Cross* (centre of triptych). Brussels

PLATE 177

Pl. 177. London (Wagner) Ecce Homo Painter: *Christ crowned with Thorns*. London N.G.

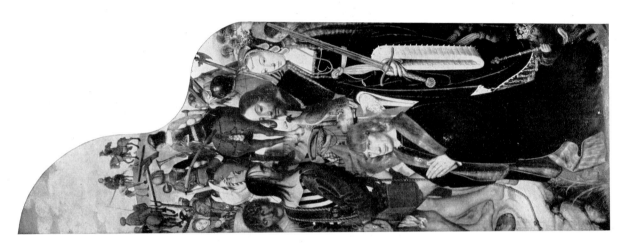

Pl. 180. Oultremont Master: *Road to Calvary with SS. Veronica, Catherine and Bavon and donor Count Albert of Adrichem (exterior wings of Pl. 176)*

Pls. 178, 179. Oultremont Master: *The Crowning with Thorns*

PLATE 181

Pl. 181. Brussels Man with a Rosary Painter: *Man with a rosary and Tiburtine Sibyl*. Brussels

PLATES 182, 183, 184, 185

Alkmaar Master: *The Seven Works of Mercy* (1504). Amsterdam Rijks.

Pl. 182. *Feeding the Hungry*   Pl. 183. *Refreshing the Thirsty*

Pl. 184. *Releasing the Captives*   Pl. 185. *Visiting the Sick*

Pl. 186. London S. Luke Painter: *S. Luke painting the Virgin*. London N.G.

. 188. Alkmaar Master: *Clothing the Naked* (detail). Amsterdam Rijks.

Pl. 187. L. van Leyden: *The Sermon* (*m*). Amsterdam Rijks.

Pl. 189. L. van Leyden: *Temptation of S. Anthony* (*m* and 1511). Brussels

PLATE 190

Pl. 190. Munich S. Helena and Constantine Painter: *S. Helena and the Emperor Constantine.* Munich

Pl. 191. Antwerp Adoration Master: *S. George* (wing of Pl. 193). Antwerp

Pl. 192. Antwerp Adoration Master: *S. Margaret and donor* (wing of Pl. 193). Antwerp

PLATE 193

Pl. 193. Antwerp Adoration Master: *Adoration of the Magi* (centre of triptych). Antwerp

PLATE 194

Pl. 194. J. Gossaert: *Adoration of the Magi* (*s*). London N.G.

PLATE 195

Pl. 195. G. David: *Virgin and Child with SS. Catherine, Agnes, Dorothy, Barbara Godelieve and Lucy (doc. 1509)*. Rouen

Pl. 199. Bruges Baptism of Christ Painter: *Madeleine second wife of donor J. des Trompes with daughter and S. Mary Magdalene* (exterior wing of Pl. 218). Bruges

Pl. 198. Hoogstraeten Master: *Jesus among the Doctors.* Antwerp

Pl. 197. Hoogstraeten Master: *Presentation in the Temple.* Antwerp

Pl. 196. Bruges Baptism of Christ Painter: *Virgin and Child* (exterior wing of Pl. 218). Bruges

Pl. 200. J. Patinir: *S. John preaching in the Wilderness* (detail of Pl. 216)

Pl. 201. Bruges Baptism of Christ Painter: *S. John preaching in the Wilderness* (detail of Pl. 218)

Pl. 201A. New York Rest on the Flight Painter: *Rest on the Flight*. New York Met.

PLATES 202, 203, 204

Pl. 202. Lisbon Alexander VI Painter: *S. Christopher*
(wing of triptych). Lisbon

Pl. 203. Dublin Flight Painter: *Flight into Egypt*. Dublin N.G.I.

Pl. 204. London Virgin with Nun Painter:
Virgin and Child with a Cistercian nun. London N.G.

PLATE 205

Pl. 205. Brussels Virgin with a Milk Bowl Painter: *Virgin and Child with a bowl of milk*. Brussels

Pl. 205A. London Virgin with Nun Painter: *Virgin and Child with a Cistercian nun*. London N.G. (*cf.* Pl. 204)

PLATE LVII.

PLATE 206

Pl. 206. Bruges Baptism of Christ Painter: *The four daughters of Elizabeth, first wife of J. des Trompes*
(detail of wing of Pl. 218). Bruges.

PLATE 207

Pl. 207. Q. Massys: *S. Anne Altarpiece, The Holy Kinship* (*s* 1509). Brussels

PLATE 208

Pl. 208. Chicago Man with a Pink Painter: *Portrait of a man*. Chicago

PLATE 209

Pl. 209. Frankfort Master: *Allegory of Death* (wings closed on triptych). Frankfort Staedel.

Pls. 210, 211. C. Engelbrechtsz: *Donors with SS. Cecilia, Mary Magdalene, James and Martin*
(wings of Pl. 213). Leyden

Pl. 212. Amsterdam Cadaver Painter: *Allegory; Vanity of Human Life*. Amsterdam Rijks.

Pl. 213. C. Engelbrechtsz: *Lamentation* (*doc.*) (centre of triptych). Leyden

Pl. 214. Frankfort Master: *Donor Claus Humbrecht with three sons* (detail of wing). Frankfort Staedel.

Pl. 215. Frankfort Master: *Donor's wife with three daughters* (detail of wing). Frankfort Staedel.

Pl. 216. J. Patinir: *Baptism of Christ* (*s*). Vienna Kunsthist.

Pl. 217. Philadelphia Lamentation Painter: *Lamentation*.
Philadelphia

Pl. 218. Bruges Baptism of Christ Painter: *Baptism of Christ*
(centre of triptych). Bruges

PLATE 219

Pl. 219. Amsterdam Delft Painter: *Holy Family with SS. Dorothy, and Catherine and angels in a walled garden* (centre of triptych). Amsterdam Rijks.

PLATE 220

Pl. 220. Amsterdam Delft Painter: *The Annunciation* (wings closed on Pl. 219). Amsterdam Rijks.

Pl. 223. London Delft Painter: *Christ presented to the people* (wing of Pl. 224). London N.G.

Pl. 222. London Passion Scenes Painter: *Christ presented to the people.* London N.G.

Pl. 221. London Delft Painter: *Descent from the Cross* (wing of Pl. 224). London N.G.

Pl. 224. London Delft Painter: *The Crucifixion* (centre of triptych). London N.G.

Pl. 225. London Delft Painter: *The Betrayal* (detail of Pl. 224)

PLATE 226

Pl. 226. London Delft Painter: *The impenitent thief with Christ carrying the Cross and the suicide of Judas.* (detail of Pl. 224)
London N.G.

Pl. 227. Amsterdam Delft Painter: *Donor with bishop as patron saint* (wing of Pl. 219). Amsterdam Rijks.

Pl. 228. Amsterdam Delft Painter: *Wife of donor with S. Barbara* (wing of Pl. 219). Amsterdam Rijks.

PLATE 229

Pl. 229. C. Engelbrechtsz: *Christ stripped. Christ mocked. Cadaver* (*doc.*) (wings closed on Pl. 232). Leyden

Pl. 230. C. Engelbrechtsz: *The Brazen Serpent*
(wing of Pl. 232). Leyden

Pl. 231. Oultremont Master: *Christ presented to the people*
(wing of Pl. 176). Brussels

PLATE 232

Pl. 232. C. Engelbrechtsz: *The Crucifixion* (*doc.*) (centre of triptych). Leyden

Pl. 233. C. Engelbrechtsz: *Detail of Pl. 232*

Pl. 234. London Delft Painter: *Detail of Pl. 224*

PLATE 235

Pl. 235. Q. Massys: *The banker and his wife* (s and 1514). Paris Louvre

Pl. 236. Bruges Death and the Miser Painter: *Compact between Death and the Miser*. Bruges

Pl. 237. Marinus van Reymerswaele: *S. Jerome in his study* (*s* and 1521). Madrid

Pl. 238. J. Gossaert: *S. Luke drawing the Virgin* (*s*). Prague Rudolfinum

Pl. 239. Brussels Haneton Lamentation Painter:
Philippe Haneton and seven sons (detail of wing of Pl. 279).
Brussels

Pl. 240. Brussels Haneton Lamentation Painter:
Margaret, wife of Philippe Haneton, and five daughters
(detail of wing of Pl. 279). Brussels

Pl. 241. J. Patinir and Q. Massys: *Temptation of S. Anthony* (s) (*Figures doc.* to Q. Massys). Madrid

Pl. 242. Vienna Catherine Painter:
Portrait of a lady with a necklace (*Catherine of Aragon?*).
Vienna Kunsthist.

Pl. 243. Brussels Young Knight Painter:
Young Knight of the Golden Fleece. Brussels

Pl. 244. J. Patinir: *Landscape with Flight into Egypt* (*s*). Antwerp

Pl. 245. J. Patinir: *Landscape with S. Jerome and the lion* (*s*). Madrid

PLATE 246

Pl. 246. J. Patinir: *Detail of Pl. 245*

PLATE 247

Pl. 247. J. Gossaert: *Neptune and Amphitrite* (*s* and 1516). Berlin K.F.

PLATE 248

Pl. 248. B. van Orley: *Virgin and Child with S. Joseph and angels* (*s* and 1522). Madrid

PLATE 249

Pl. 249. Brighton Assumption of the Virgin Painter: *Assumption of the Virgin*. Brighton

Pl. 250. A. Cornelis: *Coronation of the Virgin with choirs of angels* (*doc.* 1517–1519). Bruges S. Jacques

Pls. 251, 252, 253. A. Bouts: *Assumption of the Virgin, donors and saints*—triptych (*s* with rebus). Brussels

Pl. 256. B. van Orley:
Death of the rich man; The rich man in Hell
(wing of Pl. 257). Brussels

Pl. 255. J. Gossaert:
The Virgin of Louvain (doc.).
Madrid

Pl. 254. B. van Orley:
The rich man dining; Lazarus at the rich man's door
(wing of Pl. 257). Brussels

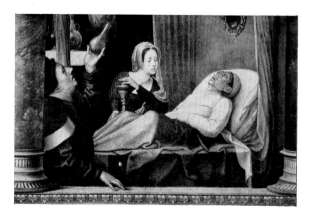

Pl. 257. B. van Orley: *The Virtue of Patience* (triptych) (*s* and 1521). *The banquet of Job's children* (centre). Brussels

Pl. 258. B. van Orley: *Detail of Pl. 254*   Pl. 259. B. van Orley: *Detail of Pl. 256*

Pl. 261. Magdalene Legend Master: *S. Mary Magdalene preaching*. Philadelphia

Pl. 260. Fogg S. Luke Painter: *S. Luke painting the Virgin*. Cambridge (Mass.) Fogg

Pl. 264. Saint Sang Master:
S. Joseph of Arimathea (wing of triptych).
Bruges: Confrérie du Saint Sang

Pl. 263. Deipara Virgo Master:
Virgin with Prophets and Sibyls. Antwerp

Pl. 262. Saint Sang Master:
S. Mary Magdalene (wing of triptych).
Bruges: Confrérie du Saint Sang

PLATE 265

Pl. 265. J. Cornelisz van Oostsanen; *Salome with the head of S. John the Baptist* (*m* and 1524). The Hague

Pl. 266. Hampton Court Cromatius Painter:
Conversion of Cromatius. Hampton Court: H.M. the Queen

Pl. 267. L. van Leyden: *The Annunciation* (*m* and 1522).
Munich

Pl. 268. J. Cornelisz van Oostsanen: *Saul and the Witch of Endor* (*m* and 1526). Amsterdam Rijks.

Pl. 269. Bruges Birth of the Virgin Painter: *Birth of the Virgin*. Bruges

Pl. 270. L. Blondeel: *S. Damian* (detail of wing of Pl. 272).
Bruges S. Jacques

Pl. 271. L. Blondeel: *S. Cosmas* (detail of wing of Pl. 272).
Bruges S. Jacques

PLATE 272

Pl. 272. L. Blondeel: *Martyrdom of SS. Cosmas and Damian* (*s* and 1523) (centre of triptych). Bruges S. Jacques

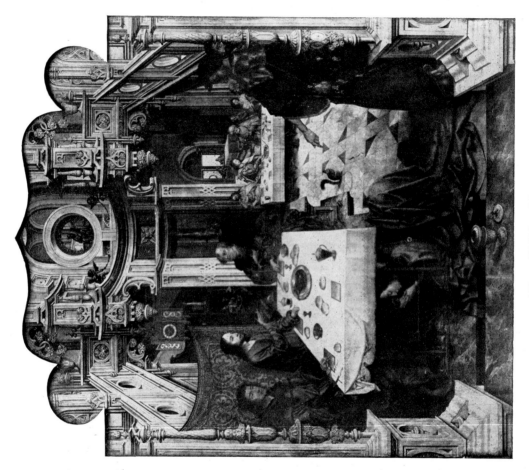

Pl. 275. *Assumption of the Magdalene*
(wing of Pl. 274). Brussels

Abbey of Dilighem Master
Pl. 274. *Christ in the house of Simon.*
Brussels

Pl. 273. *Raising of Lazarus*
(wing of Pl. 274). Brussels

Pl. 276. C. van Coninxloo: *Genealogy of the Virgin* (*s* and 1526). Brussels

Pl. 277. L. van Leyden: *Virgin and Child with S. Mary Magdalene and donor* (*m* and 1522). Munich

Pl. 280. C. de Coter: *The three Maries* (s)
Paris Louvre

Pl. 279. Brussels Haneton Lamentation
Painter: *Lamentation*
(centre of triptych). Brussels

Pl. 278. A. Benson: *Holy Family* (m)
(wing of triptych). Brussels

Pl. 281. Seven Sorrows of the Virgin Master: *The Virgin with the Seven Sorrows* (*Mater Dolorosa*). Bruges Notre Dame

Pl. 282. B. van Orley: *Last Judgement* (*doc*. 1518–1525) (detail). Antwerp

Pl. 283. J. Provoost: *Last Judgement* (*doc*. and 1525). Bruges

Pl. 284. J. van Scorel: *Baptism of Christ* (*doc*.). Haarlem

PLATE 285

Pl. 285. Detroit Crucifixion Painter: *The Crucifixion*. Detroit

Pl. 288. Solomon Master:
Jehovah rebuking Solomon
(wing of Pl. 287). The Hague

Pl. 287. Solomon Master:
Idolatry of Solomon.
The Hague

Pl. 286. Solomon Master:
The Queen of Sheba (wing of Pl. 287).
The Hague

PLATE 289

Pl. 289. **J.** van Coninxloo: *The Marriage Feast at Cana* (*s*). Brussels

PLATE 290

Pl. 290. L. van Leyden: *The Last Judgement* (*doc*. 1526) (centre of triptych). Leyden

Pl. 291. L. van Leyden: *Paradise* (wing of Pl. 290). Leyden   Pl. 292. L. van Leyden: *Hell* (wing of Pl. 290). Leyden

Pl. 293. L. van Leyden: *Detail of Pl. 290*

Pl. 294. J. Gossaert: *Children of Christian II of Denmark* (*doc.*). London, H.M. the Queen

Pl. 295. Ottawa Judith Painter: *Judith with the head of Holofernes*. Ottawa N.G.

Pl. 296. Grenoble Judith Painter: *Judith with the head of Holofernes*. Grenoble

PLATE 297

Pl. 297. J. Gossaert: *Danaë* (*s* and 1527). Munich

Pl. 298. Amsterdam Armed Arquebusiers Painter: *Seventeen arquebusiers of the A company in armour* (1531). Amsterdam Rijks.

Pl. 299. C. Anthonisz: *Banquet of Civic Guardsmen* (m and 1533). Amsterdam Rijks.

Pl. 300. J. van Scorel: *Twelve Jerusalem Pilgrims* (*s*). Haarlem

Pl. 301. J. van Scorel: *The painter's mistress, Agatha van Schoonhoven* (*s* and 1529). Rome, Doria

Pl. 302. J. Cornelisz van Oostsanen: *Portrait of a man* (*m* and 1533). Amsterdam Rijks.

Pl. 303. M. van Heemskerck: *The Virgin posing for S. Luke*
(s and 1532). Haarlem

Pl. 304. M. van Heemskerck: *S. Luke painting the Virgin*
(s and 1532). Haarlem

Pl. 305. J. van Hemessen: *The Prodigal Son* (s and 1536). Brussels

PLATE 306

Pl. 306. M. van Heemskerck: *Portrait of his father* (*inscribed* and 1532). New York Met.

Pl. 307. Pieter Coecke van Aelst: *The Last Supper* (*semi-doc.* and 1531). Brussels

Pl. 308. M. Coxie: *The Footwashing* (*s* and 1567). Brussels

Pl. 309. J. van Coninxloo: *Nativity (of the Virgin?)* (*s* and 1530). Brussels

Pl. 310. M. Coxie: *Nativity of the Virgin* (*doc.*). Madrid

PLATE 311

Pl. 311. Worcester Girl at Clavichord Painter: *Girl playing a clavichord*. Worcester, U.S.A.

PLATE 312

Pl. 312. Hampton Court Henry VIII (*c.* 1536) Painter: *King Henry VIII with a scroll.* Hampton Court, H.M. the Queen

PLATE 313

Pl. 313. Philadelphia Francis I Painter: *King Francis I with a glove*. Philadelphia

PLATE 314

Pl. 314. Female Half-Lengths Master: *Trio of musician ladies*. Vienna Harrach

PLATE 315

Pl. 315. J. Massys: *Judith with the head of Holofernes* (s and 1543). Boston

PLATE 316

Pl. 316. C. Massys: *Return of the Prodigal* (s and 1538). Amsterdam Rijks.

PLATE 317

Pl. 317. J. van Hemessen: *The Virgin and Child* (*s* and 1544). Stockholm

PLATE 318

Pl. 318. Marinus van Reymerswaele: *The moneychanger and his wife* (s and 1538). Madrid

Pl. 320. Antwerp 'Forties Painter:
Elizabeth, wife of G. van Schoonbeke (1544). Antwerp

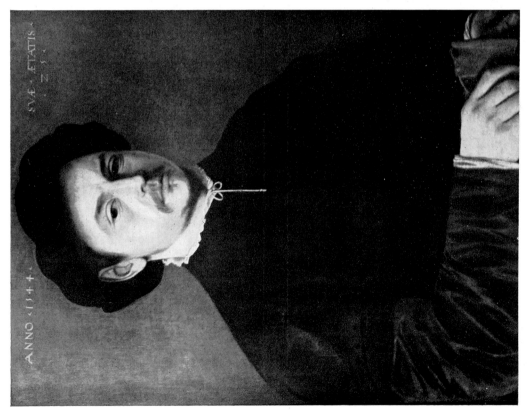

Pl. 319. 'Forties Master: *Gillis van Schoonbeke* (1544). Antwerp

Pl. 321. Brussels Micault Triptych Painter: *Jean Micault and three sons* (wing of triptych). Brussels

Pl. 322. Brussels Micault Triptych Painter: *Wife of Jean Micault and four daughters* (wing of triptych). Brussels

PLATE 323

Pl. 323. J. C. Vermeyen: *The Punishment of Ghent 1540 (s)*. Brussels Bib. Roy.

PLATE 324

Pl. 324. London Tax Collectors Painter: *Two tax collectors*. London N.G.

Pl. 325. J. van Hemessen: *The Prodigal Son* (*s* and 1543). Hartford (U.S.A.), Wadsworth Ath.

Pl. 326. Brussels Piper Painter: *Bagpiper and woman*. Brussels

PLATE 327

Pl. 327. L. Gassel: *Landscape with Judah and Tamar* (*m* and 1548). Vienna Kunsthist.

Pl. 328. L. Gassel: *Mountainous landscape with mine workers* (*m* and 1544). Brussels

Pl. 329. C. Massys: *Landscape with S. Jerome* (*m* and 1547). Antwerp

PLATE 330

Pl. 330. L. Blondeel: *S. Luke painting the Virgin* (*m* and 1545). Bruges

Pl. 331. P. J. Pourbus: *Allegorical love-feast* (*s*). London Wallace

Pl. 332. A. Mor: *Emperor Maximilian II*
(*s* and 1550). Madrid

Pl. 333. A. Mor: *Empress Maria of Austria*
(*s* and 1551). Madrid

PLATE 334

Pl. 334. P. J. Pourbus: *Last Judgement* (*m* and 1551). Bruges

PLATE 335

Pl. 335. F. Floris: *Fall of the Rebel Angels* (*m* and 1554). Antwerp

Pl. 337. P. J. Pourbus: *Wife of Jan Fernaguut* (s and 1551). Bruges

Pl. 336. P. J. Pourbus: *Jan Fernaguut* (s and 1551). Bruges

PLATE 338

Pl. 338. H. Ewouts: *Mary Nevill, Baroness Dacre* (*m*). Ottawa N.G.

Pl. 339. Paris Granvella's Dwarf Painter:
Cardinal Granvella's dwarf with dog. Paris Louvre

Pl. 341. A. Mor: *Bishop (later Cardinal) Granvella* (s and 1549).
Vienna Kunsthist.

Pl. 340. C. van Hemessen: *Portrait of a man* (s and 1552).
London N.G.

Pl. 342. A. Mor: *Catherine of Austria, Queen of Portugal*
(doc. 1552). Madrid

Pl. 343. A. van Cronenburch: *Lady in Dutch dress* (s). Madrid

Pl. 345. C. van Hemessen: *Lady with a little dog* (s and 1551). London N.G.

Pl. 344. London Lady in a Flat Cap Painter: *Portrait of a young lady*. London N.G.

Pl. 346. C. van Hemessen: *Portrait of a lady* (s). Barnard Castle

PLATE 347

Pl. 347. Madrid Philip II (Head) Painter: *King Philip II*. Madrid

PLATE 348

Pl. 348. G. Mostaert: *Christ on the Cross* (*s*). Copenhagen

PLATES 349, 350

Pl. 350. H. Ewouts: *Henry Stuart, Lord Darnley with his brother Charles Stuart later Earl of Lennox* (m and 1563). Windsor: H.M. the Queen

Pl. 349. H. Ewouts: *Queen Mary* (m and 1554). London Soc. of Antiquaries

Pl. 350A. A. Mor: *Queen Mary of England* (*s* and 1554). Madrid

Pl. 351. F. Floris: *S. Luke painting* (*m* and 1556). Antwerp   Pl. 352. M. Coxie: *S. Cecilia* (*s*). Madrid

Pl. 353. F. Floris: *Feast of the Sea gods* (*m* and 1561). Stockholm

PLATE 354

Pl. 354. M. van Heemskerck: *Aaron and Moses with the brazen serpent* (s and 1551). Haarlem

PLATE 355

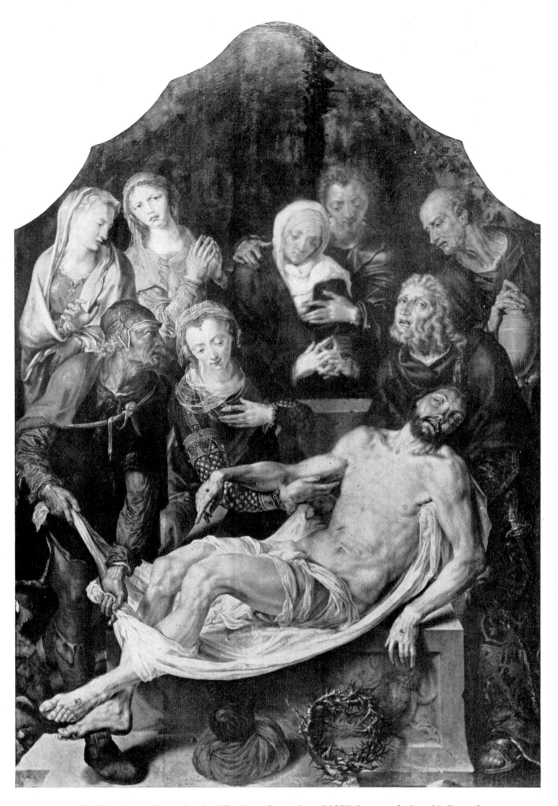

Pl. 355. M. van Heemskerck: *The Entombment* (*s* and 1559) (centre of triptych). Brussels

Pl. 356. P. Aertsen: *Market scene with Christ and the adulteress* (*m* and 1559). Frankfort Staedel.

Pl. 357. P. Aertsen: *Christ in the house of Mary and Martha* (*m* and 1559). Brussels

Pl. 358. Brussels Prodigal Son Painter: *The Prodigal Son* (*m* Hb).
Brussels

Pl. 359. Brussels Kitchen Scene Painter:
Kitchen scene with cook and boy. Brussels

Pl. 360. P. Aertsen: *Kitchen scene* (*m* and 1562). Stockholm

Pl. 361. J. Massys: *The Holy Family turned away from the inn*
(s and 1558). Antwerp

Pl. 362. J. Massys: *The healing of Tobit* (s and 1564).
Antwerp

Pl. 363. J. Massys: *Flora* (s and 1561). Stockholm

Pl. 364. M. de Vos: *Apollo and the Muses* (s). Brussels

Pl. 365. M. van Heemskerck: *Self portrait with the Colosseum* (s and 1553). Cambridge Fitz.

PLATE 366

Pl. 366. P. van der Hofstadt: *An old man in prayer* (s and 156–). Vienna Liecht.

PLATE 367

Pl. 367. P. de Kempener: *Descent from the Cross* (*doc.* 1561). Montpellier

PLATE 368

Pl. 368. P. Bruegel: *Detail of Pl. 375*

Pl. 368A. P. Bruegel: *Detail of Pl. 370*

Pl. 369. P. Bruegel: *Children's games* (s and 1560). Vienna Kunsthist.

Pl. 370. P. Bruegel: *Battle between Carnival and Lent* (s and 1559). Vienna Kunsthist.

PLATE 371

Pl. 371. F. Mostaert: *Landscape with the Good Samaritan* (s). Antwerp

Pl. 372. M. van Heemskerck: *Christ on the Sea of Tiberias* (s and 1567). Barnard Castle

Pl. 373. Brussels Icarus Painter: *Landscape with fall of Icarus*. Brussels

Pl. 374. L. van Valkenborch: *Tower of Babel* (*m* and 1594). Paris Louvre

Pl. 375. P. Bruegel: *Tower of Babel* (*s* and 1563). Vienna Kunsthist.

PLATE 376

Pl. 376. J. de Punder: *Portrait of a Bishop* (s and 1563). Baltimore (U.S.A.)

Pl. 377. T. van Haecht: *Landscape with hunting adventure of Archduke Maximilian in the Tyrol* (*m* and 1615).
Brussels

Pl. 378. P. Bruegel: *Suicide of Saul* (*s* and 1562 (?)). Vienna Kunsthist.

Pl. 378A. P. Bruegel: *Conversion of S. Paul (s* and 1567). Vienna Kunsthist.

Pl. 379. P. Bruegel: *The Road to Calvary* (s and 1564). Vienna Kunsthist.

Pl. 380. P. Brueghel the younger: *The Road to Calvary* (s and 1603). Antwerp

Pl. 382. P. Bruegel: *Massacre of the Innocents* (s) (detail). Vienna Kunsthist.

Pl. 381. P. Bruegel: *Detail of Pl. 379*

PLATE 383

Pl. 383. P. Bruegel: *Adoration of the Magi* (s and 1564). London N.G.

Pl. 384. Chicago 1562 Painter: *Portrait of a lady* (1562). Chicago Art Inst.

Pl. 386. C. de Zeeu: *Bearded man in a cap* (*s* and 1563). Amsterdam Rijks.

Pl. 385. C. de Zeeu: *Man in a red chair* (*s* and 1565). Oxford S. John's College

Pl. 387. W. Key: *Old woman* (*s*). Amsterdam Rijks.

Pl. 388. Amsterdam Moucheron Family Painter: *Pierre de Moucheron, his wife Isabeau and their twenty children* (1563). Amsterdam Rijks.

Pl. 389. D. Barendsz: *Fourteen Civic guardsmen* (*doc.* and 1562). Amsterdam Rijks.

Pl. 390. P. Bruegel: *The dark day* (*March? or Spring?*) (*s* and 1565). Vienna Kunsthist.

Pl. 391. P. Bruegel: *Hunters in the snow* (*February? or Winter?*) (*s* and 1565). Vienna Kunsthist.

Pl. 392. P. Bruegel: *The harvesters* (*July? or Summer?*) (*s* and '65). New York Met.

Pl. 393. P. Bruegel: *Return of the herd* (*November? or Autumn?*) (*s* and 1565). Vienna Kunsthist.

PLATE 394

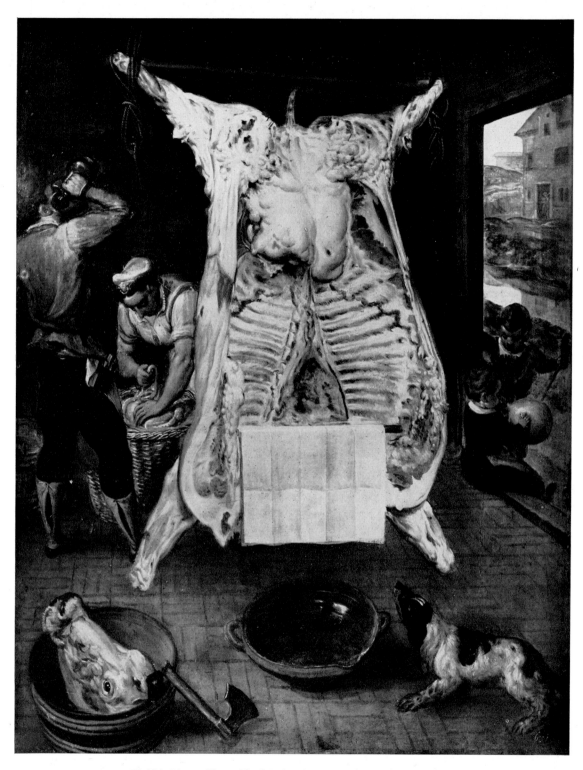

Pl. 394. M. van Cleve: *The flayed ox* (*m* and 1566). Vienna Kunsthist.

Pl. 395. Prodigal Son Master: *Story of the Prodigal Son*. Vienna Kunsthist.

Pl. 396. M. van Cleve: *Peasant household and cavalier* (*doc*.). Vienna Kunsthist.

Pl. 397. M. de Vos: *S. Paul at Ephesus; The burning of the books* (*s* and 1568). Brussels

Pl. 398. J. Beuckelaer: *Fishmarket with Ecce Homo* (*s* and 1570). Stockholm

Pl. 399. J. Beuckelaer: *Kitchen scene with Christ in the house of Mary and Martha* (*m* and 1565). Stockholm

Pl. 400. J. Beuckelaer: *S. Anne and the Holy Kinship* (*m* and 1567). Copenhagen

PLATE 401

Pl. 401. M. Helmon: *Adoration of the Shepherds* (*s*). New York Met.

Pl. 402. L. van Noort: *Adoration of the Shepherds* (*m* and 1568). Brussels

Pl. 403. M. Coffermans: *Penitent Magdalene* (*s* and 1568). Madrid

Pl. 404. Detroit Wedding Dance Painter: *The Wedding Dance*. Detroit

Pl. 405. P. Bruegel: *Peasant wedding* (*doc.*). Vienna Kunsthist.

Pl. 406. M. van Cleve: *The brawl* (*doc.*). Vienna Kunsthist.

Pl. 407. P. Bruegel: *Peasant dance* (*s*). Vienna Kunsthist.

PLATE 408

Pl. 408. A. Mor: *Anne of Austria, Queen of Spain* (*s*). Vienna Kunsthist.

PLATE 409

Pl. 409. C. van den Broeck: *Last Judgement* (*s* and 1571). Antwerp

Pl. 410. Madrid Triumph of Death Painter: *The Triumph of Death*. Madrid

Pl. 411. P. Brueghel the younger or J. (Velvet) Brueghel: *The Triumph of Death* (s and 1597). Vienna Liecht.

PLATE 412

Pl. 412. P. Huys: *Battle of angels and demons and torments of Hell* (s and 1570). Madrid

Pl. 413. P. Huys: *Temptation of S. Anthony* (*s* and 1577). Antwerp, Mayer van den Bergh Mus.

Pl. 414. P. Bruegel: *The Land of Cockayne* (*s* and 1567). Munich

Pl. 415. Madrid Triumph of Death Painter: *Detail of Pl. 410*

Pl. 416. J. de Backer: *Last Judgement* (s and 1571). Antwerp

Pl. 417. H. Ewouts: *The Wise and Foolish Virgins* (*m* and 1570). Copenhagen

Pl. 418. Dublin Rebecca Painter: *Rebecca at the well*. Dublin N.G.I.

Pl. 419. Vienna Feast of the Gods Painter: *Feast of the Gods*. Vienna Kunsthist.

Pl. 420. A. Blocklandt van Montfoort: *Diana and Actaeon* (*m* and 1573). Vienna Kunsthist.

PLATE 421

Pl. 421. P. Pietersz: *Shadrach, Meshach and Abednego in the Fiery Furnace* (*m* and 1575). Haarlem

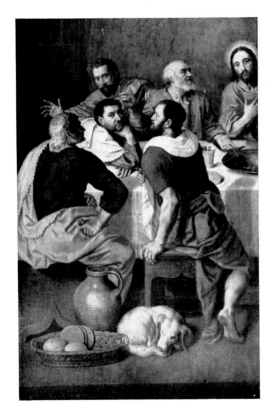 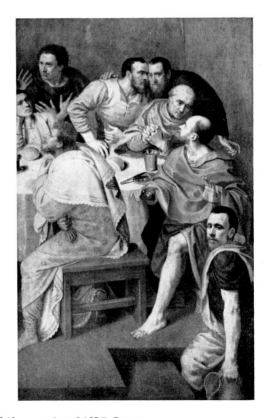

Pl. 422. A. Claeissins: *Banquet of Ahasuerus* (*s* and 1574). Bruges

A. Key: *Last Supper* (*s*). Antwerp
Pls. 423 and 424. *Exterior wings of triptych* (*cf.* Pls. 425 and 426)

Pl. 425. A. Key: *Gillis de Smidt, syndic of the Antwerp Recollets convent, with seven children (s and 1575). Antwerp*

Pl. 426. A. Key: *Maria de Deckere, second wife of Gillis de Smidt, and daughter (s). Antwerp*

(cf. Pls. 423 and 424)

Pl. 427. F. Pourbus the elder: *Duke of Alençon* (?) (s and 1574).   Pl. 428. A. Mor: *Gentleman with a dog* (s and 1569).
London Wallace   Washington N.G.

Pl. 429. M. de Vos: *The Antwerp shipowner Gilles Hoffman and his wife* (s and 1570). Amsterdam Rijks.

PLATE 430

Pl. 430. J. Grimmer: *Outskirts of Antwerp (Kiel) with peasants and covered waggons* (s and 1578). Antwerp

Pl. 431. H. Bol: *Panorama of Antwerp* (*s* and 1575). Brussels

Pl. 432. L. van Valkenborch: *Landscape with village* (*m* and 1570). Brussels

Pl. 433. Antwerp Destruction of Citadel Painter: *Demolition of the Spanish Citadel in Antwerp 1577*. Antwerp

Pl. 434. G. Congnet: *S. George* (*s* and 1581). Antwerp

Pl. 435. Worcester Destruction of Citadel Painter: *Demolition of the Spanish Citadel in Antwerp 1577*. Worcester, U.S.A.

Pl. 436. P. Claeissins the younger: *The Convention of Tournai; (Allegory of the Spanish Triumph)* (*s* and 1584). Bruges

PLATE 437

Pl. 437. A. Key: *Portrait of a man* (*m* and 1580). Brussels

Pl. 438. J. Savery the elder: *Landscape with Jephtha's daughter* (*s* and 158–). Amsterdam Rijks.

Pl. 439. M. van Valkenborch: *February; Flight into Egypt* (*m*). Vienna Kunsthist.

Pl. 440. J. W. Delff: *Reconciliation of Jacob and Esau* (s and 1584). Vienna Kunsthist.

Pl. 441. A. van Cronenburch: *Lady holding a yellow flower* (s). Madrid

Pl. 442. G. Congnet: *Pierson la Hues, drummer of the Crossbowmen* (s). Antwerp

PLATE 443

Pl. 443. A. van Cronenburch: *Young lady with a girl holding carnations* (s and 1587). Madrid

Pl. 444. J. Grimmer: *Landscape with castle* (*s* and 1583). Vienna Kunsthist.

Pl. 445. L. van Valkenborch: *Autumn* (*fruit gathering*) (*m* and 1585). Vienna Kunsthist.

Pl. 446. L. van Valkenborch: *Spring (picnic with elegant company)* (*m* and 1587). Vienna Kunsthist.

Pl. 447. A. Grimmer: *Landscape with castle* (*The Fortune teller*) (*s* and 1592). Brussels

PLATE 448

Pl. 448. L. van Valkenborch: *The Gergesene Demoniacs* (*m* and 1597). Brussels

Pl. 449. L. van Valkenborch: *Landscape with ironworks* (*m*). Madrid

Pl. 450. L. van Valkenborch: *Mountain landscape* (*m* and 1582). Amsterdam Rijks.

Pl. 451. C. Ketel: *The Company of Captain Rosencranz and Lieutenant Pauw* (*s* and 1588). Amsterdam Rijks.

Pl. 452. Amsterdam Little Girl with dog Painter: *Little Girl with dog* (1581). Amsterdam Rijks.

Pl. 453. H. van der Mast: *Portrait of a lady* (*m* and 1587). Amsterdam Rijks.

PLATE 454

Pl. 454. G. Geldorp: *Hortensia del Prado* (*m* and 1596). Amsterdam Rijks.

PLATE 455

Pl. 455. O. van Veen: *Mystic marriage of S. Catherine* (*s* and 1589). Brussels

PLATE 456

Pl. 456. H. de Clerck: *The Lineage of S. Anne* (*s* and 1590). Brussels

Pl. 458. B. Spranger: *Hercules and Omphale* (s).
Vienna Kunsthist.

Pl. 457. Joos van Winghe: *Apelles painting Campaspe* (s).
Vienna Kunsthist.

PLATE 459

Pl. 459. B. Spranger: *Allegory of the virtues of Rudolf II* (*m* and 1592). Vienna Kunsthist.

PLATE 460

Pl. 460. J. Snellinck ; *The Crucifixion* (*s* and 1597). Antwerp

PLATE 461

Pl. 461. J. Tiel: *Allegory of the education of Philip III* (*s*). Madrid

PLATE 462

Pl. 462. J. V. de Vries: *Musical party in a loggia* (s and 1596). Vienna Kunsthist.

Pl. 462A. London Queen Elizabeth at Ditchley Painter: *Queen Elizabeth at Ditchley*. London N.P.G.

PLATE 463

Pl. 463. Hampton Court Lady in a Persian dress Painter: *Arabella Stuart (?) in Persian dress with a stag.*
Hampton Court: H.M. the Queen

PLATE 464

Pl. 464. J. (Velvet) Brueghel: *Landscape with Tobias and hunting party* (s and 1598). Vienna Liecht.

Pl. 465. J. (Velvet) Brueghel: *Latona and the peasants* (s and 1601). Frankfort Staedel.

Pl. 466. G. van Coninxloo: *Wooded landscape with huntsman crossing bridge* (s and 1598). Vienna Liecht.

PLATE 467

Pl. 467. J. (Velvet) Brueghel: *Village fair* (s and 1600). Windsor: H.M. the Queen

Pl. 468. P. Stevens the younger: *Village fair* (*m* and 1596). Antwerp

Pl. 469. A. Mirou: *Landscape with Abraham and Hagar* (*s*). Madrid

Pl. 470. J. (Velvet) Brueghel: *Adoration of the Magi* (*s* and 1598). Vienna Kunsthist.

Pl. 471. H. de Clerck: *Suffer little children to come unto me* (*s* and 1592) (detail). Brussels

PLATE 472

Pl. 472. K. van Mander: *Jesus leaving the Temple with his parents* (*m* and 1598). Vienna Kunsthist.

PLATE 473

Pl. 473. P. Brill: *Rocky landscape* (s and 1602). Glasgow

Pl. 474. P. Brill: *Italian landscape with ruins* (s). Amsterdam Rijks.

Pl. 475. W. van Nieulandt: *View of Rome* (s and 1611). Antwerp

Pl. 476. G. van Coninxloo: *Wooded landscape* (*m* and 1604). Vienna Liecht.

Pl. 477. H. de Clerck and D. van Alsloot: *Wooded landscape with Cephalus and Procris* (*s* and 1608).
Vienna Kunsthist.

Pl. 478. A. Govaerts: *Oakwood with gipsies* (*s* and 1612). The Hague

Pl. 479. A. van Stalbemt: *Wooded landscape with hunters and dogs* (*s*). Amsterdam Rijks.

Pl. 480. J. (Velvet) Brueghel: *Village on river bank* (*s* and 1604). Amsterdam Rijks.

Pl. 481. J. (Velvet) Brueghel: *River landscape* (*The Ferry*) (*s* and 1603). Antwerp

Pl. 482. J. (Velvet) Brueghel: *The road to the market* (s and 1603). Vienna Kunsthist.

Pl. 483. J. (Velvet) Brueghel: *Landscape with a covered waggon* (s and 1603). Madrid

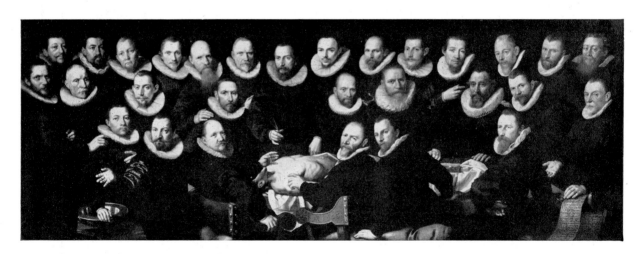

Pl. 484. J. de Gheyn: *A white Spanish warhorse* (*s* and 1603). Amsterdam Rijks.

Pl. 485. A. Pietersz: *Anatomy lecture of Dr. Egbertsz* (*m* and 1603). Amsterdam Rijks.

PLATE 486

Pl. 486. G. Geldorp: *Catherine Fourmenois as a child* (*m* and 1604). Amsterdam Rijks.

PLATE 487

Pl. 487. H. van Steenwyck the younger: *Interior of a Gothic church* (s and 1605). Vienna Kunsthist.

Pl. 488. H. van Steenwyck the elder: *Night scene in a crypt* (s). Amsterdam Rijks.

Pl. 489. H. van Steenwyck the younger: *Liberation of S. Peter* (s and 1621). Vienna Kunsthist.

PLATE 490

Pl. 490. J. Uytewael: *Annunciation to the Shepherds* (*s*). Amsterdam Rijks.

Pl. 491. A. Dubois: *Baptism of Clorinda by Tancred* (*doc.*). Paris Louvre

Pl. 492. A. Claeissins: *Mars and the Fine Arts overcoming Ignorance* (*s* and 1605). Bruges

PLATE 493

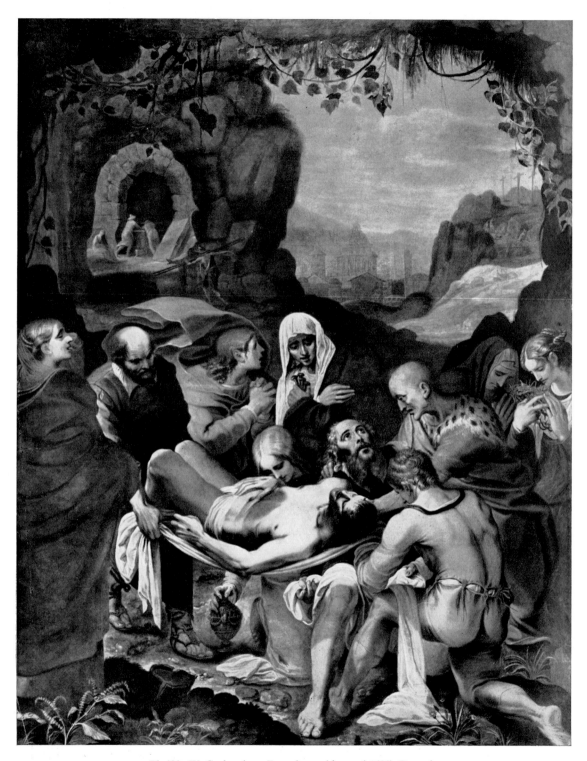

Pl. 493. W. Coebergher: *Entombment* (*doc.* and 1605). Brussels

Pl. 494. P. Schoubroeck: *Troy burning and Aeneas carrying his father* (s and 1606). Vienna Kunsthist.

Pl. 495. Brussels Sodom and Gomorrah Painter: *Destruction of Sodom and Gomorrah*. Brussels

PLATE 496

Pl. 496. F. Francken II: *Witches' Sabbath* (s and 1607). Vienna Kunsthist.

Pl. 497. Joos van Winghe: *Night banquet and masquerade* (*doc*.). Amsterdam Rijks.

Pl. 498. J. Uytewael: *Diana and Actaeon* (*s* and 1607). Vienna Kunsthist.

Pl. 499. J. Tilens: *Landscape near Tivoli* (*s*). Vienna Kunsthist.

Pl. 500. J. de Momper; *Mountain landscape* (*doc*.). Vienna Kunsthist.

Pl. 501. K. de Keuninck: *Landscape with a shipwreck and a saint* (s). Ghent

Pl. 502. F. van Valkenborch: *Mountain landscape with robbers* (s and 1605). Amsterdam Rijks.

Pl. 503. H. Francken the elder: *Still life* (s and 1607). Antwerp

Pl. 504. Clara Peeters: *Still life with fish and artichokes* (s and 1611). Madrid

Pl. 505. Grenoble Artichoke Painter: *Still life with artichoke*. Grenoble

Pl. 506. O. Beet the elder: *Still life with oysters* (s). Madrid

PLATE 507

Pl. 507. H. van Balen: *Rape of Europa* (*doc.*). Vienna Kunsthist.

Pl. 508. H. van Balen: *Pluto and Persephone* (*s*). Brighton

Pl. 509. A. Janssens: *Allegory of Antwerp and the Scheldt* (*doc.* and 1610). Antwerp

Pl. 510. O. van Veen: *Brinio acclaimed chief of the Caninifates* (*doc.* 1613). Amsterdam Rijks.

Pl. 511. O. van Veen: *Supper in the wood* (*doc.* 1613). Amsterdam Rijks.

PLATE 512

Pl. 512. P. P. Rubens: *Isabella Brant* (detail of Pl. 516)

PLATE 513

Pl. 513. D. van Alsloot: *Feast of Our Lady of the Wood (Vivier d'Oye Fête in Tervueren Forest)* (s and 1616). Madrid

PLATE 513A

Pl. 513A. D. van Alsloot: *Ommeganck procession 1615* (Detail): *The cars of Diana and Apollo and the ship-car of Charles V.* (s and 1616). London Vic. and Alb.

Pl. 514. A. Sallaert: *Procession with the maidens dowered by the Infanta Isabella 1615* (*doc.*). Brussels

Pl. 515. A. van Nieulandt: *The 1606 Procession of the lepers on 'Kopper Maandag' in Amsterdam* (*s* and 1633). Amsterdam Rijks.

PLATE 516

Pl. 516. P. P. Rubens: *P. P. Rubens and Isabella Brant* (*doc.*). Munich

Pl. 517. F. Francken II: *Ball at the Court of Albert and Isabella 1611 (s)*. The Hague

Pl. 518. H. Staben: *Visit of Archduke Albert and Infanta Isabella to Rubens' studio (s)*. Brussels

PLATE 519

Pl. 519. F. Francken: *Flagellation* (*s*). Barnard Castle

PLATE 520

Pl. 520. Munich Duchess Magdalena Painter: *Duchess Magdalena of Bavaria* (*?*). Munich

PLATE 521

Pl. 521. J. (Velvet) Brueghel: *Bouquet of flowers* (*doc.*). Vienna Kunsthist.

Pl. 522. Clara Peeters: *Still life with flowers, dried fruit and cakes* (s and 1611). Madrid

Pl. 523. Clara Peeters: *Still life with fish and shells* (s). Amsterdam Rijks.

PLATE 524

Pl. 524. J. Uytewael: *Adam and Eve* (*s* 'inventor' and 1614). Gateshead Shipley Art Gallery

Pl. 525. R. Savery: *Cow shed with milking (and witches on brooms)* (s and 1615). Amsterdam Rijks.

Pl. 526. Vienna Daniel Painter: *Daniel in the lions' den*. Vienna Kunsthist.

PLATE 527

Pl. 527. G. Seghers: *S. Theresa* (*doc.*). Antwerp

Pl. 528. P. P. Rubens: *Raising of the Cross* (*doc.* 1610–1611).
Antwerp Cathedral

Pl. 529. P. P. Rubens: *Descent from the Cross* (*doc.* 1614).
Antwerp Cathedral

Pl. 530. P. P. Rubens: *Lamentation* (*s* and 1614). Vienna Kunsthist.

Pl. 531. S. Vrancx: *Attack on a convoy* (*s*) and 1616). Windsor: H.M. the Queen

Pl. 532. S. Vrancx: *Horse market* (*m*). Brussels

Pl. 533. D. Vinckeboons: *Flemish fair* (*m* and 1610). Antwerp

Pl. 534. S. Vrancx: *Market place with flogging and a funeral* (*m*). Amsterdam Rijks.

PLATE 535

Pl. 535. A. Grimmer: *Christ in the house of Mary and Martha* (s and 1614). Brussels

Pl. 536. H. van Steenwyck the younger: *Open square with figures* (*m* and 1614). The Hague

Pl. 537. H. van Steenwyck the younger: *Christ in the house of Mary and Martha* (*s* and 1620). Paris Louvre

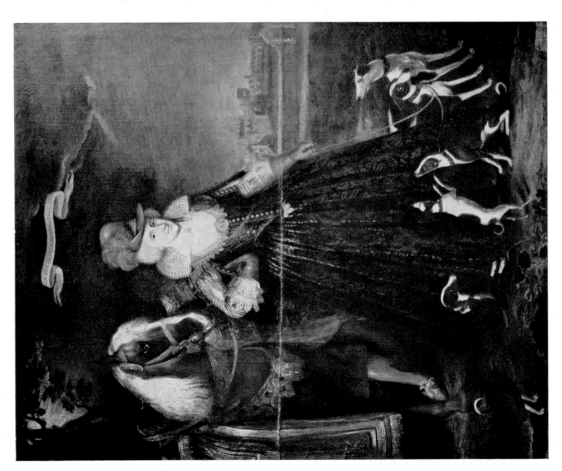

Pl. 539. F. Pourbus the younger: *Marie de Médicis* (s and 1617). Madrid

Pl. 538. P. van Somer: *Anne of Denmark, Queen of James I, with horse, negro and dogs* (s and 1617). Windsor: H.M. the Queen

PLATE 540

Pl. 540. F. Pourbus the younger: *Isabella of Bourbon, first Queen of Philip IV* (*doc.*). Madrid

PLATE 541

Pl. 541. J. (Velvet) Brueghel and P. P. Rubens: *The Virgin and Child in a garland of flowers* (*doc.*). Paris Louvre

Pl. 542. J. (Velvet) Brueghel: *The Five Senses; (Sight)* (*s* and 1617). Madrid

Pl. 543. J. (Velvet) Brueghel and P. P. Rubens: *Adam and Eve in Paradise* (*s* by both). The Hague

PLATE 544

Pl. 544. P. P. Rubens (and assistants): *Nature adorned by the Graces* (*doc.*). Glasgow

Pl. 545. J. Jordaens: *Allegory of Abundance* (*s*). Brussels

Pl. 546. J. Jordaens: *The daughters of Cecrops finding Erichthonius* (*s* and 1617). Antwerp

PLATE 547

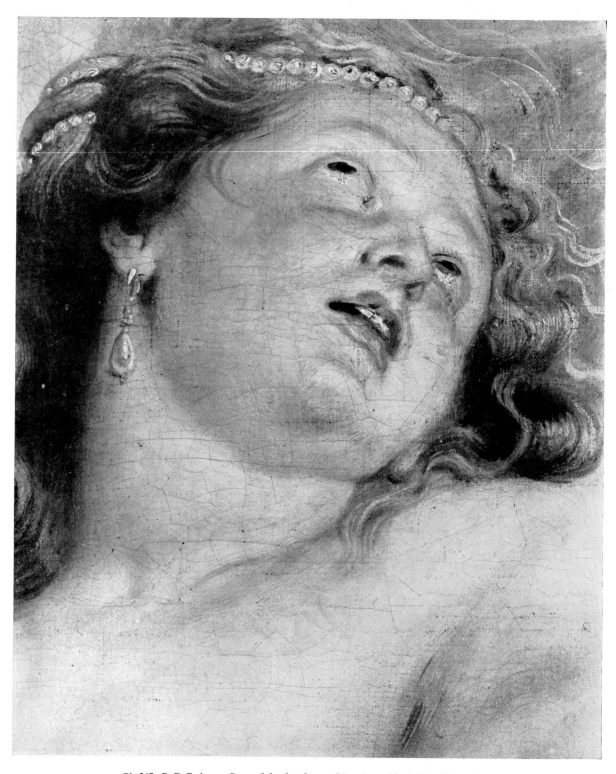

Pl. 547. P. P. Rubens: *Rape of the daughters of Leucippus* (*doc.*). (detail) Munich

Pl. 547A. P. P. Rubens: *Rape of the daughters of Leucippus* (*doc.*). Munich

Pl. 548. P. P. Rubens (and assistants): *Cimon finding the sleeping Iphigenia* (*doc.*). Vienna Kunsthist.

Pl. 549. *Detail of Pl. 548*

PLATE 550

Pl. 550. Ambrosius Bosschaert: *Flowers in a faience vase* (*m* and 1619). Amsterdam Rijks.

Pl. 551. Ambrosius Bosschaert: *Glass of flowers in a niche*
(*m* and 1618). Copenhagen

Pl. 552. Ambrosius Bosschaert: *Flowers on window sill* (*m*).
The Hague

Pl. 553. Grenoble Strawberry Painter: *Still life with strawberries and flowers*. Grenoble

Pl. 554. F. Snyders: *Termes: and garland round a bust of Ceres* (*s*). Philadelphia

Pl. 555. F. Snyders: *Still life with fruit and game* (*s*). Amsterdam Rijks.

Pl. 556. J. van Hulsdonck: *Basket of fruit* (s). Barnard Castle

Pl. 557. J. van Es: *Grapes* (s). Barnard Castle

Pl. 558. J. van Es: *Still life with fish* (*s*). Frankfort Staedel.

Pl. 559. A. Adriaenssen: *Still life with cheese, bread and fish* (*s*). Madrid

PLATE 560

Pl. 560. London van der Geest Painter : *Cornelius van der Geest*. London N.G.

Pl. 561. L. van Uden: *River landscape with sunset* (*m*). Antwerp

Pl. 562. A. van Stalbemt: *Wooded landscape with fables* (*s* and 1620). Antwerp

Pl. 563. J. Fouquier: *River landscape* (s and 1620). Nantes

Pl. 564. R. Savery: *Stag and boar hunt in a rocky landscape* (s and 1620). Amsterdam Rijks.

Pl. 565. P. P. Rubens: *Flat landscape with an avenue of trees* (*doc.*). Boston (U.S.A.)

Pl. 566. L. van Uden: *Flat landscape with peasants* (*s*). Vienna Kunsthist.

Pl. 567. L. van Uden: *Wooded landscape with peasants dancing* (figures by D. Teniers *m*) (*s*). Dublin N.G.I.

Pl. 568. P. P. Rubens (and assistants): *Summer* (*doc*.). Windsor: H.M. the Queen

Pl. 571. M. Pepyn: *Poor family going to hospital (s)* (wing of Pl. 572) exterior. Antwerp

Pl. 570. O. van Veen: *The Charity of S. Nicholas (doc.)*. Antwerp

Pl. 569. M. Pepyn: *S. Elizabeth tending the sick (s)* (wing of Pl. 572) exterior. Antwerp

PLATE 572

Pl. 572. M. Pepyn: *S. Elizabeth giving her jewels to the poor* (*s*) (centre of triptych). Antwerp

PLATE 573

Pl. 573. P. de Lignis: *Adoration of the Magi* (*s* and 1616). Madrid

PLATE 574

Pl. 574. P. P. Rubens: *Adoration of the Magi* (*doc.* 1624). Antwerp

PLATE 575

Pl. 575. P. P. Rubens: *Marie de Médicis* (*doc.*). Madrid

Pl. 576. P. P. Rubens: *Battle of the Amazons* (*doc.*). Munich

Pl. 577. P. P. Rubens: *The flight of Lot* (*s* and 1625). Paris Louvre

PLATE 578

Pl. 578. P. P. Rubens: *Arrival of Marie de Médicis at Marseilles (sketch) (doc.)*. Munich

PLATE 579

Pl. 579. A. van Dyck: *Elena Grimaldi, Marchesa Cattaneo* (*doc.*). Washington N.G.

PLATE 580

Pl. 580. Hague Studio of Apelles Painter: *The Studio of Apelles; Interior of a picture gallery.* The Hague

Pl. 581. T. Rombouts: *Card players* (*doc.*). Madrid

Pl. 582. Madrid Judith Painter: *Judith and servant with the head of Holofernes*. Madrid

Pl. 583. R. Savery: *Birds in a forest* (s). Antwerp

Pl. 584. I. van Oosten: *The Garden of Eden* (s). Vienna Liecht.

Pl. 585. R. Savery: *Fable of the Hart and the Cows* (*s*). Amsterdam Rijks.

Pl. 586. R. Savery: *Orpheus charming the animals* (*s* and 1628). London N.G.

PLATE 587

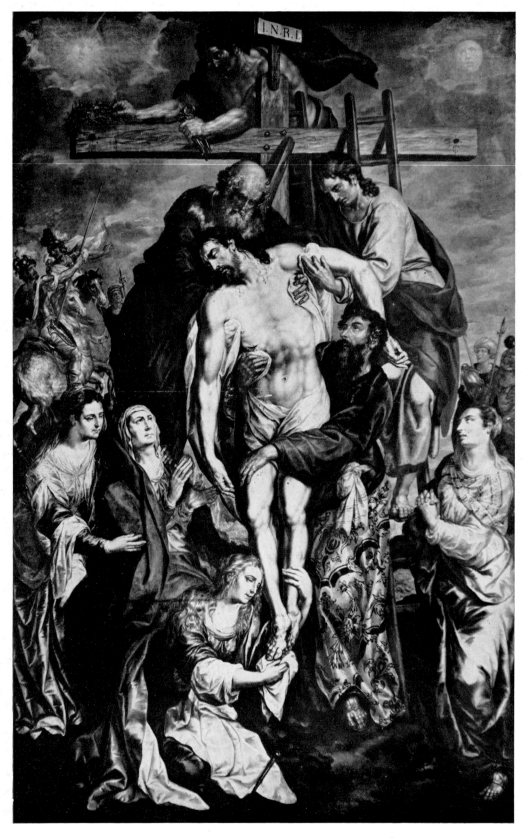

Pl. 587. H. de Clerck: *Descent from the Cross* (*m* and 1628). Brussels

Pl. 588. J. Jordaens: *S. Martin curing a demoniac* (s and 1630). Brussels

Pl. 589. T. van Thulden: *Young lord renouncing the world* (s). Brussels.

Pl. 590. C. de Vos: *Apollo and the Python* (s) (detail). Madrid

PLATE 591

Pl. 591. P. P. Rubens: *Helena Fourment in her wedding dress* (*doc.* 1630). Munich

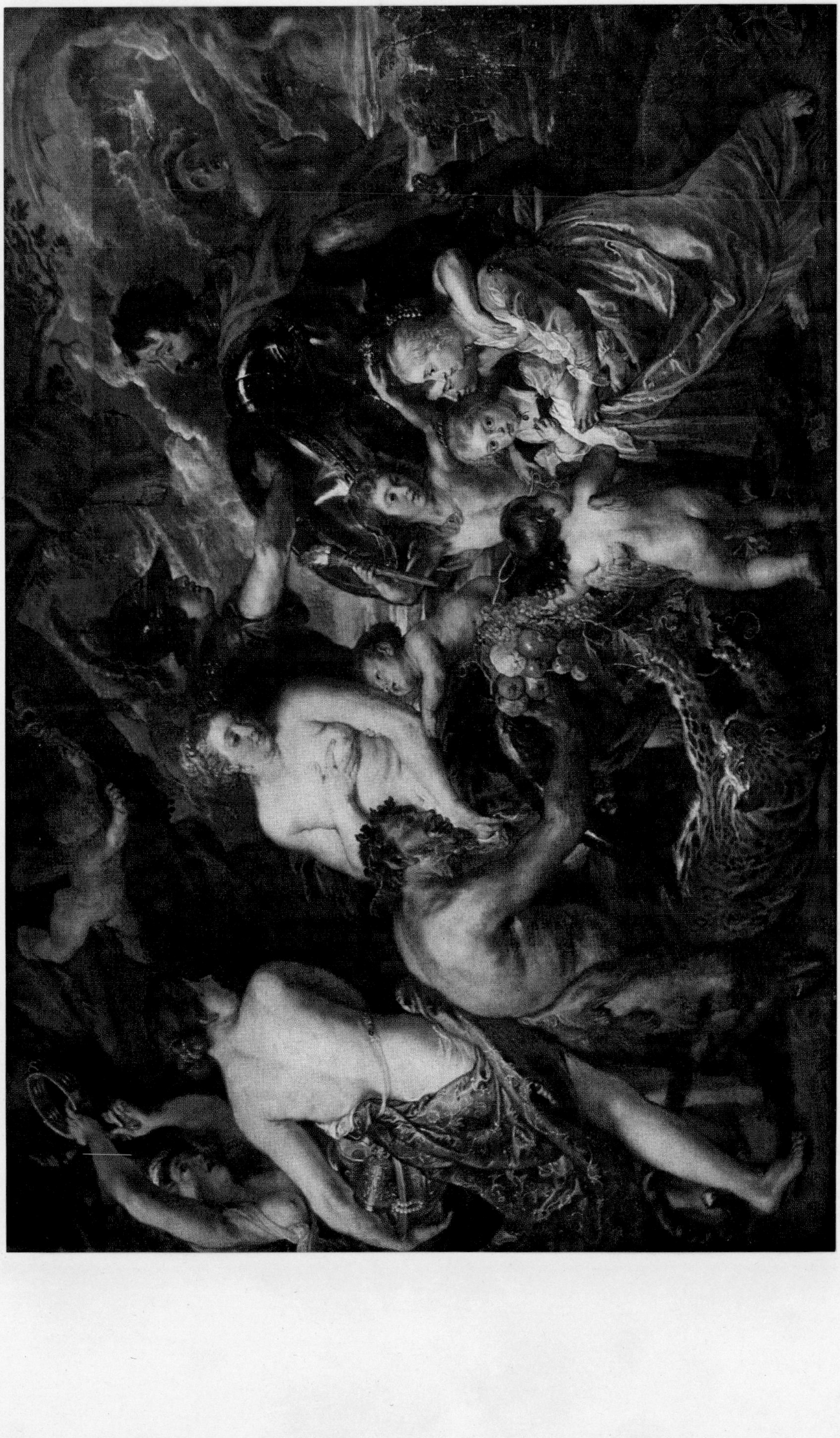

Pl. 591A. P. P. Rubens: *Peace and War (doc.)* London N.G.

Pl. 592. J. van Reyn: *Marriage of Peleus and Thetis* (*m* and 163–). Madrid

Pl. 593. J. de Paepe: *Venus and Adonis* (*s* and 1629). Amsterdam Rijks.

Pl. 594. G. Backereel: *Hero and Leander* (*doc.*). Vienna Kunsthist.

PLATE 595

Pl. 595. A. Brouwer: *The Smoker* (*m*). Paris Louvre

Pl. 596. T. Rombouts: *The Quack Dentist* (*doc.*). Madrid

Pl. 597. T. Rombouts: *Christ driving the moneychangers from the Temple* (*s*). Antwerp

PLATE 598

Pl. 598. G. de Crayer: *The Virgin protecting the Crossbowmen's Guild* (*doc.*). Brussels

Pl. 599. C. de Vos: *S. Norbert recovering the Sacred Vessels* (*s* and 1630). Antwerp

Pl. 600. C. de Vos: *Family group* (*s* and 1631). Philadelphia

PLATE 601

Pl. 601. P. P. Rubens: *Helena Fourment nude with a fur coat* (*doc.*). Vienna Kunsthist.

Pl. 602. L. van Uden: *Flat landscape with peasants and horses* (*s*). Frankfort Staedel.

Pl. 603. P. P. Rubens (and assistants): *Landscape with cattle* (*doc.*). Munich

PLATE 604

Pl. 604. A. van Dyck: *Venus and Vulcan* (*doc.*). Paris Louvre

Pl. 605. P. van Avont and J. Brueghel the younger: *Flora in a garden* (*s* by both). Vienna Kunsthist.

Pl. 606. A. Wolfordt: *Rest on the Flight* (*m*). Madrid

PLATE 607

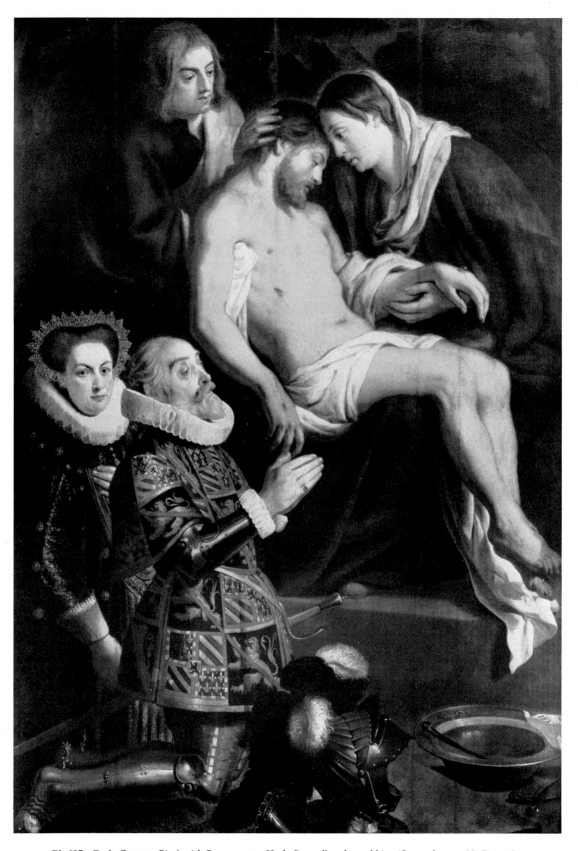

Pl. 607. G. de Crayer: *Pietà with Burgomaster H. de Dongelberghe and his wife as adorants (s)*. Brussels

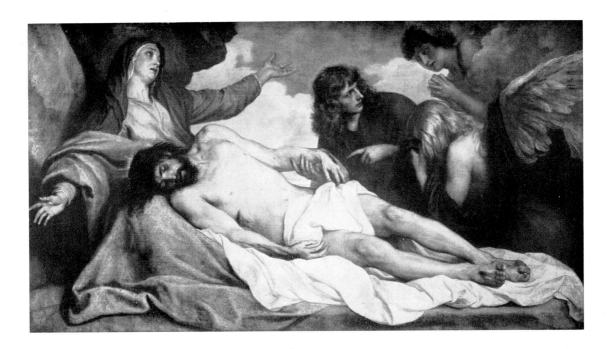

Pl. 608. A. van Dyck : *Lamentation* (*doc.*). Antwerp

Pl. 609. G. de Crayer : *Lamentation* (*doc.*). Vienna Kunsthist.

Pl. 610. A. Keirincx: *Landscape with bathing women* (*m*). Copenhagen

Pl. 611. A. Keirincx: *Oakwood with stag hunt* (*s* and 1630). Antwerp

PLATE 612

Pl. 612. A. van Dyck: *Philip, Lord Wharton* (*s* and 1632). Washington N.G.

PLATE 613

Pl. 613. A. Keirincx: *Landscape with shepherd (s)*. Brussels

Pl. 614. A. Goubau: *Farmyard with figures* (s). Dublin N.G.I.

Pl. 615. V. Malo: *Peasants before an inn* (m). Amsterdam Rijks.

PLATE 616

Pl. 616. J. van Craesbeeck: *Landscape with soldiers and women* (*m*). Vienna Kunsthist.

Pl. 617. A. Brouwer: *Peasants' and soldiers' brawl by wayside inn* (*m*). Amsterdam Rijks.

Pl. 618. A. Brouwer: *Boors' carouse* (*m*). Amsterdam Rijks.

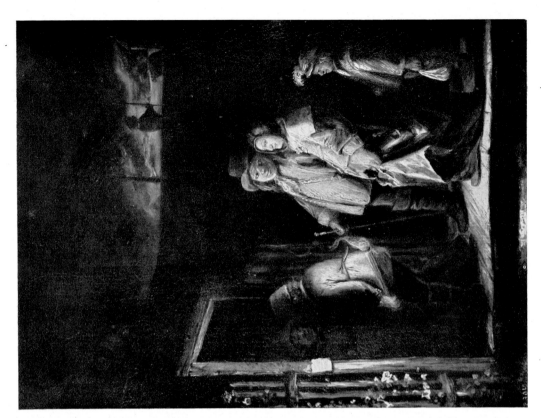

Pl. 620. J. van Craesbeeck: *Homecoming by night (m)*.
Vienna Liecht.

Pl. 619. J. van Craesbeeck: *The lute player (Prodigal Son) (m)*.
Vienna Liecht.

Pl. 622. London Wallace Sleeping Boor Painter : *Pipe drunkard (Boor asleep).* London Wallace

Pl. 621. Munich Tobacco Den Painter : *Interior of a tobacco den.* Munich

PLATE 623

Pl. 623. A. Brouwer: *Peasants and Spanish soldiers at a table in the grounds of Antwerp citadel (s)*. Brussels

Pl. 624. A. Victoryns: *Peasant interior* (*s*). Copenhagen

Pl. 625. A. Brouwer: *Outdoor dentistry* (*m*). Vienna Liecht.   Pl. 626. J. van Craesbeeck: *Boors' concert* (*m*). Madrid

PLATE 627

Pl. 627. P. Snayers: *Hunting scene; Philip IV killing a wild boar* (*s*). Madrid

Pl. 628. J. Wildens: *View of Antwerp from the countryside* (*s* and 1636). Amsterdam Rijks.

Pl. 629. J. Wildens: *Landscape with dancing peasants* (*s* and 1631). Antwerp

PLATE 630

Pl. 630. F. Snyders: *The Fable of the Hare and the Tortoise* (*s*). Madrid

PLATE 631

Pl. 631. P. P. Rubens: *Wrath of Neptune* (`*Quos Ego*') (doc.). *Detail of sketch for panel in triumphal arch for Pageant Entry into Antwerp of Cardinal Infante Ferdinand 1635*. Cambridge Mass. Fogg Mus.

Pl. 634. F. Snyders: *Decorative panel with wild cat, monkey, fox and ermines* (s). Madrid

Pl. 633. P. de Vos: *Greyhound in flat landscape* (s). Madrid

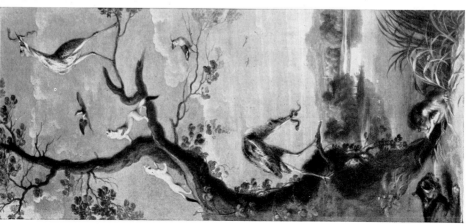

Pl. 632. F. Snyders: *Decorative panel with waterbirds and ermines* (s). Madrid

Pl. 635. F. Snyders: *Stag hunt* (s). Brussels

Pl. 636. P. de Vos: *Stag hunt* (s). Madrid

Pl. 637. J. Gowi: *Hippomenes and Atalanta* (*s*). Madrid

Pl. 638. P. Symons: *Cephalus spied upon by Procris* (*s*). Madrid

Pl. 639. E. Quellinus: *Bacchus and Ariadne* (*s*). Madrid   Pl. 640. J. Cossiers: *Narcissus* (*s*). Madrid

Pl. 641. C. de Vos: *Triumph of Bacchus* (*s*). Madrid

Pl. 643. P. P. Rubens: *Cardinal Infante Ferdinand at the Battle of Nordlingen 1634 (doc.).* Madrid

Pl. 642. G. de Crayer: *Cardinal Infante Ferdinand (s and 1639).* Madrid

PLATE 644

Pl. 644. A. van Dyck: *Charles I with horse, equerry and groom* (*s*). Paris Louvre

Pl. 645. C. de Baellieur: *Visit to an art gallery* (*s* and 1637). Paris Louvre

Pl. 646. D. Ryckaert III: *A painter in his studio* (*s* and 1638). Paris Louvre

Pl. 647. A. van Nieulandt: *Amphitrite* (*s* and 1651). Amsterdam Rijks.

Pl. 648. F. Francken II: *Neptune and Amphitrite* (*s*). Madrid

Pl. 649. P. Neeffs the elder: *Church interior with candle light effect* (*s* and 1636). Amsterdam Rijks.

Pl. 650. P. Neeffs the elder: *Interior of Antwerp Cathedral* (*s* and 1638). Boston (U.S.A.)

PLATE 651

Pl. 651. J. van Reyn: *Lady in black dress with red ribbons* (s and 1637). Brussels

Pl. 652. A. Adriaenssen: *Still life with cod, salmon, other fish and a cat (s)*. Madrid

Pl. 653. A. Adriaenssen: *Still life with lobster, haddock and other fish (s and 1660)*. Amsterdam Rijks.

PLATE 654

Pl. 654. P. Franchoys: *Young man with a wine glass* (*Le rubis sur l'ongle*). (*s* and 1639). Brussels

PLATE 655

Pl. 655. F. Snyders: *The market stall* (*doc.*). Hartford (U.S.A.) Wadsworth Ath.

Pl. 656. F. Snyders: *Larder with swan and servant* (*s*). Brussels

Pl. 657. F. Snyders: *Larder with swan, asparagus and young man in kitchen* (*s*). Ottawa N.G.

PLATE 658

Pl. 658. J. Jordaens: *Twelfth Night* (*Le roi boit*) (*doc.*). Vienna Kunsthist.

Pl. 659. Paris Expulsion of Traders Painter: *Christ driving the traders from the Temple*. Paris Louvre

Pl. 660. J. Jordaens: *The old sing and the young pipe* (*s* and 1638). Antwerp

Pl. 661. P. P. Rubens: *Young people disporting in a castle park* (*doc.*). Vienna Kunsthist.

Pl. 662. P. P. Rubens: *The Garden of Love* (*Fête galante*). Madrid

PLATE 663

Pl. 663. A. van Dyck: *Diana Cecil, Countess of Oxford* (*s* and 1638). Madrid

PLATE 664

Pl. 664. P. P. Rubens: *Landscape with Atalanta hunting (doc.).* Brussels

Pl. 668a. P. P. Rubens: *Peasant dance* (*doc.*) Madrid (*cf.* Pl. 666)

Pl. 665. P. P. Rubens: *Kermesse* (*doc.*). Paris Louvre

Pl. 666. P. P. Rubens: *Peasant dance* (*doc.*). Madrid

Pl. 667. F. Wouters: *Landscape with Venus and Adonis* (*m*). Copenhagen

Pl. 668. W. Panneels: *Diana and her nymphs* (*s* and 1640). Nantes

Pl. 669. C. Schut: *Bacchus and his train* (*doc.*). Vienna Kunsthist.

Pl. 670. P. P. Rubens: *The Judgement of Paris* (*doc.*). Madrid

Pl. 671. E. Quellinus: *The Queen of Sheba before Solomon* (*s*). Vienna Liecht.

Pl. 672. T. Willeboirts (Bosschaert): *Venus arming Mars* (*Allegory of Prince Frederick Henry 1644*) (*s*). Amsterdam Rijks.

Pl. 673. S. de Vos: *The beheading of S. Paul* (*s* and 1648). Antwerp

Pl. 674. S. de Vos: *Gipsy woman telling young man's fortune* (*s* and 1639). Antwerp

PLATE 675

Pl. 675. J. A. van der Baren: *Flowers round a mystic marriage of S. Catherine* (*s*). Brussels

Pl. 676. P. van der Plas: *The Virgin and Child with syndics of a Brussels Guild* (s and 1647). Brussels

Pl. 677. P. van Lint: *The Pool of Bethesda* (s and 1642). Brussels

PLATE 678

Pl. 678. D. Teniers the younger: *Kitchen scene with swan pâté* (*s* and 1644), The Hague

Pl. 679. D. Teniers the younger: *The goatherd* (s). Vienna Kunsthist.

Pl. 680. D. Teniers the younger: *Boors' carouse* (s and 1644). London Wallace

Pl. 681. J. Teniers the younger: *Interior with old woman peeling apples* (*s*). Copenhagen

Pl. 682. D. Teniers the younger: *Interior with old woman peeling apples* (*s*). Cambridge Fitz.

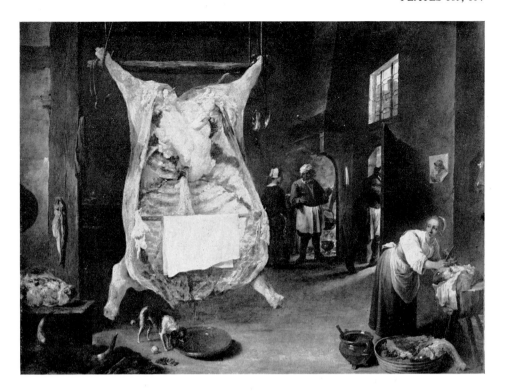

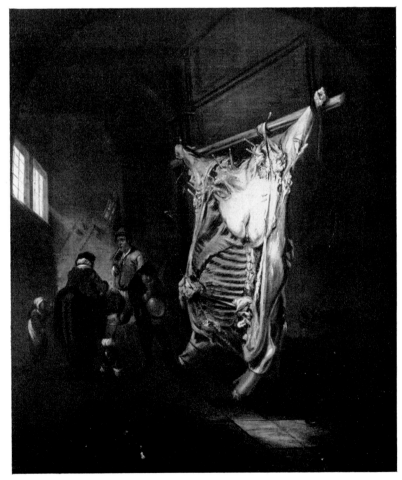

Pl. 683. D. Teniers the younger: *The flayed ox* (s). Boston (U.S.A.)

Pl. 684. A. van den Hecken: *The flayed ox* (s). Amsterdam Rijks.

Pl. 685. L. de Vadder: *Wooded landscape with peasants* (*m*). Barnard Castle

Pl. 686. J. d'Arthois: *The road through the woods* (*s*). Boston (U.S.A.)

PLATE 687

Pl. 687. S. de Vos: *A lady with a dish of fruit* (*s*). Barnard Castle

Pl. 688. A. Willaerts: *Coast scene with stormy sea and ships* (*m* and 1638). Frankfort Staedel

Pl. 689. B. Peeters the elder: *The Scheldt with shipping round a pier* (*m*). Amsterdam Rijks.

Pl. 690. B. Peeters the elder: *Stormy sea and shipwreck* (*m*). Brussels

Pl. 691. Jan Peeters: *Stormy sea and shipwreck* (*m*). Vienna Kunsthist.

PLATE 692

Pl. 692. D. Seghers: *Garland of flowers round a statue of the Virgin* (*s* and 1645). The Hague

Pl. 693. A. van Utrecht: *Still life with food, musical instruments, monkey, parrot and dog* (s and 1644). Amsterdam Rijks.

Pl. 694. A. van Utrecht: *Fruit garland* (s and 1640). Brussels

Pl. 695. F. Ijkens: *Still life with hare, asparagus and dead birds* (s and 1646). Madrid

Pl. 696. C. Luyckx: *Cat and birds* (s). Antwerp

PLATE 697

Pl. 697. P. van Lint: *Portrait of a baby with a rattle and a dog* (s and 1645). Antwerp

Pl. 698. P. Meulener: *Cavalry skirmish* (s and 1644). Madrid

Pl. 699. L. de Hondt the elder: *Horsemen in pursuit of baggage waggon* (s). Frankfort Staedel

Pl. 700. P. Snayers: *Spanish troops besieging the French in Courtrai 1648* (*s* and 1650). Brussels

Pl. 701. P. Snayers: *Cavalry skirmish* (*s* and 1646). Madrid

PLATE 702

Pl. 702. B. Peeters: *Dutch men-of-war off a West Indian coast* (m and 1648). Hartford (U.S.A.) Wadsworth Ath.

Pl. 703. G. van Eyck: *Naval battle between Turks and Maltese* (*s* and 1649). Madrid

Pl. 704. A. van Ertvelt: *Harbour with Spanish warships* (*m*). Vienna Kunsthist.

Pl. 705. D. Ryckaert III: *Peasants' distress (Soldiers plundering a village)* (s and 1649). Vienna Kunsthist.

Pl. 706. D. Teniers the younger: *Soldiers plundering a village* (s and 1648). Vienna Kunsthist.

Pl. 707. D. Teniers the younger: *Château with figures and a greyhound* (*s*). Montpellier

Pl. 708. D. Teniers the younger: *Village fête with cauldrons* (*Fête aux chaudrons*) (*s* and 1643) (detail). London N.G.

Pl. 709. D. van Heil: *Skating scene* (*m*). Brussels

Pl. 710. J. d'Arthois: *Winter landscape* (*s*). Brussels

Pl. 711. R. van den Hoecke: *Skating on Brussels moat* (*m* and 1649). Vienna Kunsthist.

Pl. 712. D. Teniers the younger: *Archduke Leopold Wilhelm Shooting at the Popinjay in Brussels 1651* (*s* and 1652). Vienna Kunsthist.

Pl. 713. D. van Heil: *Conflagration near Antwerp* (*m*). Brussels

Pl. 714. D. van Heil: *Conflagration* (*m* and 1655). Brussels

PLATE 715

Pl. 715. J. van Oost the elder: *Boy with a muff* (*m* and 1650). London N.G.

Pl. 716. J. van den Hoecke: *May and June; Tapestry design* (*doc.*). Vienna Kunsthist.

Pl. 717. P. Thys: *Allegory of Night; Tapestry design* (*doc.*). Vienna Kunsthist.

Pl. 718. P. Thys: *Allegory of Day; Tapestry design* (*doc.*). Vienna Kunsthist.

Pl. 719. J. Fyt and T. Willeboirts (Bosschaert) : *Diana returning from the chase* (*s* and 1650. *doc.* to T.W.). Vienna Kunsthist.

Pl. 720. J. Boeckhorst: *Mercury enamoured of Herse* (*doc.*). Vienna Kunsthist.

Pl. 721. J. van den Hoecke: *Archduke Leopold Wilhelm on horseback* (*doc.*). Vienna Kunsthist.

Pl. 722. J. van Egmont: *Archduke Leopold Wilhelm* (*doc.*).
Vienna Kunsthist.

Pl. 723. P. Thys: *Archduke Leopold Wilhelm* (*doc.*).
Vienna Kunsthist.

Pl. 724. D. Teniers the younger: *Archduke Leopold Wilhelm in his picture gallery at Brussels 1651* (s and 1651). Brussels

Pl. 725. D. Teniers the younger: *Archduke Leopold Wilhelm in his picture gallery at Brussels with the Conde de Fuensaldaña,*
the artist and others (s). Madrid

PLATE 726

Pl. 726. D. Teniers the younger: *Archduke Leopold Wilhelm in his picture gallery at Brussels with the dwarfish Court Chaplain, Canon J. A. van der Baren and others (doc.)*. Vienna Kunsthist.

Pl. 727. C. de Baellieur: *Adoration of the Magi* (*s*). Brussels

Pl. 728. F. Francken III: *Family group in a picture gallery* (*s*). Antwerp

PLATE 729

Pl. 729. J. van Oost the elder: *S. Martin dividing his cloak* (*s*). Bruges

Pl. 730. H. Janssens: *Ball at the court of Don John of Austria* (*s* and 1658). Lille

Pl. 731. H. Janssens: *La main chaude* (*s* and 1656). Brussels

Pl. 732. J. van Kessel the elder: *Birds and dead fox* (*s* and 1660). Madrid

Pl. 733. J. Fyt: *Dogs and waterfowl* (*s*). Madrid

Pl. 734. D. de Coninck: *Hawk and dogs attacking waterfowl* (*s*). Amsterdam Rijks.

Pl. 735. A. de Gryef: *Eagle attacking poultry* (*s*). Brussels

Pl. 736. J. d'Arthois: *Lake with trees and horsemen* (*m*). Frankfort Staedel.

Pl. 737. A. van der Meulen: *Halt of horsemen* (*s*). Montpellier

Pl. 738. I. van der Stock : *Wooded landscape with figures* (*s* and 1661). Brussels S. Gudule

Pl. 739. F. Coppens : *Wooded landscape with Holy Family* (*s*). Brussels Notre Dame de la Chapelle

PLATE 740

Pl. 740. J. van Oost the elder: *Christ crowned with thorns* (*s* and 1661). Bruges

Pl. 741. J. Jordaens: *Adoration of the Shepherds* (*s* and 1653). Frankfort Staedel.

Pl. 742. P. de Champaigne: *Mother Catherine Agnes Arnauld and the artist's daughter Sister Catherine de S. Suzanne* (*s* and 1662).
Paris Louvre

Pl. 743. Joris van Son: *Still life with oysters, fruit and butterfly* (*s* and 1664). Madrid

Pl. 744. A. Coosemans: *Still life with fruit and asparagus* (*s*). Madrid

Pl. 745. Joris van Son: *Still life with oysters, fruit and flowers*
(*s* and 1664). Madrid

Pl. 746. Abraham Brueghel: *Still life with pomegranates and
white grapes* (*s* and 1670). Amsterdam Rijks.

Pl. 747. T. Aenvanck: *Still life with grapes and other fruit* (*s* and 1653). Antwerp

Pl. 748. C. de Heem: *Table with watch, oysters and fruit* (*s*). Vienna Kunsthist.

PLATE 749

Pl. 749. J. D. Coosemas: *Still life with peaches, grapes and glass of white wine* (*s*). Madrid

PLATE 750

Pl. 750. P. de Champaigne : *Louis XIV conferring the Order of the S. Esprit on the Duc d'Anjou* (*s* and 1665). Grenoble

Pl. 751. J. Ijkens: *Allegory in honour of the birth of a prince* (*s* and 1659). Antwerp

Pl. 752. J. Huysmans: *Queen Catherine of Braganza as Shepherdess with cupids* (*doc.*). Windsor: H.M. the Queen

Pl. 753. T. van Thulden: *Love and Music* (*s* and 1652). Brussels

Pl. 755. G. Gysaerts: *Flower garland round grisaille portrait of H. van Weert* (s). Amsterdam Rijks.

Pl. 754. J. P. van Thielen: *Flower garland round a bust of Flora* (s and 1665). Amsterdam Rijks.

Pl. 756. A. Bosman: *Flower garland round a sculptured high*   Pl. 757. D. Seghers: *Flower garland round a sculptured shield* (*s*).
  relief (*s* and 1659). Copenhagen   Copenhagen

Pl. 758. N. van Verendael: *Flowers round an antique bust* (*s*). Brussels

PLATE 759

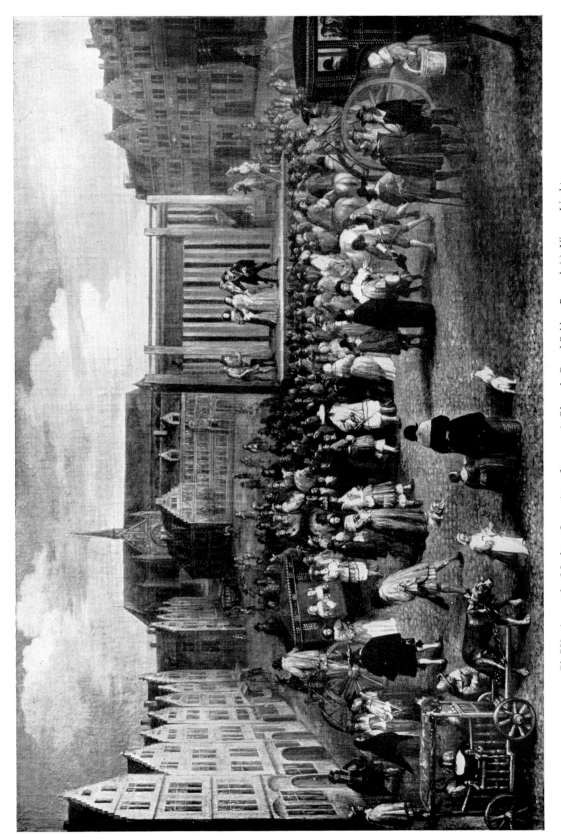

Pl. 759. A. van der Meulen: *Open air performance in Place du Grand Sablon, Brussels* (s). Vienna Liecht.

Pl. 760. G. van Schoor: *L'Hôtel de Nassau at Brussels* (*s* and 1658). Brussels

Pl. 761. H. Janssens: *Family group* (*The betrothal*) (*s*). Vienna Liecht.

PLATE 762

Pl. 762. G. van Tilborgh : *Family group with young lady at a harpsichord* (s). Brussels

Pl. 763. G. van Tilborgh: *Family group round a dining table* (*s*). The Hague

Pl. 764. G. Coques: *The Verbiest family on a terrace* (*s* and 1664). London: H.M. the Queen

Pl. 765. E. de Bie: *Place de Meir, Antwerp, with coaches and promenaders* (*s*). Antwerp

Pl. 766. A. van der Meulen: *Hunting party with coach* (*s* and 1662). London N.G.

PLATE 767

Pl. 767. V. Boucquet: *The standard bearer* (s and 1664). Paris Louvre

PLATE 768

Pl. 768. M. Sweerts: *In the studio; young artists with plaster casts* (s and 1652). Detroit

Pl. 769. J. van Oost the younger: *Jacques Matyn, canon of Bruges S. Donatien (s).* Brussels

Pl. 770. W. Vaillant: *Young artist drawing from a cast (doc.).* London N.G.

Pl. 771. J. van Oost the younger: *Children drawing from a cast (s and 1666).* Bruges

PLATE 772

Pl. 772. J. Miel: *Roman Carnival* (*s* and 1653). Madrid

Pl. 773. G. Coques: *Interior of a picture gallery* (*doc.*). The Hague

Pl. 774. J. Jordaens: *Commerce and Industry protecting the Fine Arts* (*doc.* 1665). Antwerp

PLATE 775

Pl. 775. A. Goubau: *Artists drawing antiques in the Roman Campagna* (s and 1662). Antwerp

Pl. 776. A. Goubau: *Piazza Navona, Rome* (s and 1680). Antwerp

Pl. 777. F. Duchatel: *The Marquis of Castel-Rodrigo receiving the allegiance of the states of Flanders 1666* (s and 1668). Ghent

Pl. 778. P. van Bredael: *Market outside an Italian town* (*s*). Stockholm

Pl. 779. J. van Buken: *Italian market scene with actors on a stage* (*s*). Stockholm

Pl. 780. J. F. Soolmaker: *Italianate landscape with Jacob and Esau* (*s*). Brussels

Pl. 781. G. de Witte: *Fortune teller in the Roman campagna* (*s* and 1667). Antwerp

Pl. 782. A. G. Gheringh: *Interior of Antwerp Jesuit Church* (*s* and 1665). Vienna Kunsthist.

Pl. 783. W. van Ehrenberg: *Interior of Antwerp Jesuit Church* (*s* and 1667). Brussels

Pl. 784. C. E. Biset: '*William Tell*' *performed before S. Sebastian's Guild at Antwerp* (doc.). Brussels

Pl. 785. N. van Eyck: *The 1673 review of the Antwerp Guard* (s and 1673). Antwerp

Pl. 786. H. Sporckmans: *Antwerp begging the Emperor to re-open the Scheldt* (s). Antwerp

Pl. 787. J. Siberechts: *The cradle: domestic scene in the artist's house* (*s* and 1671). Copenhagen

Pl. 788. J. Siberechts: *Farmyard* (*s* and 1660) (detail). Brussels Pl. 789. J. Siberechts: *Farmyard* (*s* and 1660) (detail). Brussels

Pl. 790. J. Siberechts: *Market cart with animals at a ford* (s and 1671). Dublin N.G.I.

Pl. 791. J. Siberechts: *Peasant girls at a ford* (s and 1665). Antwerp

Pl. 792. J. Siberechts: *Peasant girls with cart and cattle at a ford* (s). Antwerp

PLATE 793

Pl. 793. H. van Minderhout: *The Port of Bruges* (s and 1653 or 1663). Bruges

Pl. 794. H. van Minderhout: *Disembarkation* (s and 1688). Madrid

Pl. 795. L. Smout the younger: *Beach scene at Scheveningen* (s). Antwerp

Pl. 796. P. Bout: *Village fair with actors on a stage* (*s* and 1676). Brussels

Pl. 797. P. Bout: *Skating scene* (*s* and 1678) (detail). Madrid

Pl. 798. M. Schoevaerdts: *The procession of the fat ox in front of the Swan Inn* (*s*). Brussels

Pl. 799. P. Gysels: *Village fair* (*s* and 1687). Antwerp

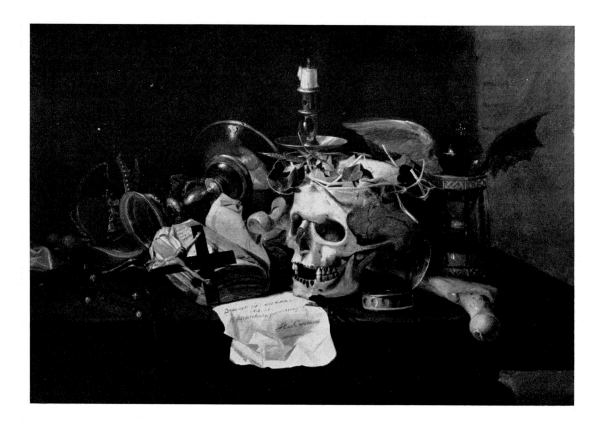

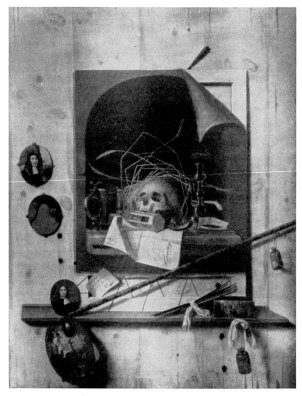

Pl. 800. A. Coosemans: *Vanitas* (*s*). Brussels

Pl. 801. Hague Vanitas Painter: *Vanitas*. The Hague   Pl. 802. C. Gysbrechts: *Vanitas* (*s* and 1668). Copenhagen

Pl. 803. C. Gysbrechts: *Still life with letter carrier on wall* (s and 1671). Copenhagen

Pl. 804. C. Gysbrechts: *Musical instruments on wall* (doc.).
Copenhagen

Pl. 805. C. Gysbrechts: *Violin and documents on wall* (s).
Copenhagen

Pl. 806. P. Gysels: *Still life with peacock, parrot and cupids in a loggia* (*s*). Antwerp

Pl. 807. Abraham Brueghel: *Young lady picking grapes* (*s*). Stockholm

Pl. 808. J. van Kessel the younger: *Family in a garden with portrait of the artist at a window* (s and 1680). Madrid

Pl. 809. G. Verbruggen the younger: *Vase of flowers with allegorical figures* (s and 1696). Antwerp

Pl. 810. G. Verbruggen the elder: *Vase of flowers with allegorical figures* (s and 1668). Antwerp

Pl. 811. J. Denys: *Allegory of the study of the nude* (*doc.* 1693). Antwerp

Pl. 812. V. Janssens: *S. Carlo Borromeo interceding for the plague-stricken* (*s*) (detail). Brussels

Pl. 813. G. de Lairesse: *Parnassus* (s) (detail). Dresden

Pl. 814. G. de Lairesse: *Achilles discovered among the daughters of Lycomedes* (s). Stockholm

Pl. 815. A. Baudewyns: *Italianate landscape with foreground figures* (s). Amsterdam Rijks.

Pl. 816. M. Schoevaerdts: *Italianate landscape with mounted figures and peasants* (s). Cambridge Fitz.

Pl. 817. A. Genoels: *Landscape with Diana hunting* (*s*). Amsterdam Rijks.

Pl. 818. J. F. van Bloemen: *Italian landscape with foreground figures* (*doc.*). Madrid

Pl. 819. J. F. van Bloemen: *Italian landscape with pastoral figures* (*s*). Glasgow

Pl. 820. J. F. van Bloemen: *The Campo Vaccino, Rome* (partially *s* and *doc*.). Madrid

PLATE 821

Pl. 821. J. E. Quellinus: *Miracle of S. Hugh, Bishop of Lincoln* (s and 1685). Antwerp

PLATE 822

Pl. 822. A. Coppens: *Self portrait with ruins of Brussels and steeple of Town Hall in background* (*s*). Brussels

Pl. 823. R. van Audenaerd: *Assembly of monks in Baudeloo Abbey, Ghent* (*doc.*). Ghent

Pl. 824. J. J. Horemans the younger: *Pageant entry of Charles of Lorraine into Antwerp in 1749* (*doc.*). Antwerp

PLATE 825

Pl. 825. J. B. Huysmans: *Landscape with cattle and two herdsmen* (s and 1697). Brussels

Pl. 826. A. Genoels: *Landscape with Minerva and the Muses* (*doc*.). Antwerp

Pl. 827. V. Janssens: *Dido building Carthage* (*s*). Brussels

Pl. 828. C. Francken: *The Battle of Eeckeren 1703* (*s* and 1703). Antwerp

Pl. 829. P. Tillemans: *Attack on a convoy* (*s*). Brussels

Pl. 830. Jan P. van Bredael: *Prince Eugene's victory over the Turks at Peterwardein, 1716 (s)*. Vienna Kunsthist.

Pl. 831. C. Breydel: *Cavalry attack (s)*. Brussels

PLATE 832

Pl. 832. B. van den Bossche: *Reception of J. B. del Campo, Burgomaster of Antwerp, at the headquarters of the Junior Guild of Crossbowmen (s and 1711).* Antwerp

Pl. 833. G. Thomas: *A painter's studio* (*s*). Antwerp

Pl. 834. I. van der Beken: *Portrait group on the terrace of a park* (*s* and 1722). Copenhagen

PLATE 835

Pl. 835. J. Horemans: *Interior with figures* (s). Amsterdam Rijks.

Pl. 836. J. Horemans the elder: *The Shoemaker's shop* (*s* and 1712). Vienna Kunsthist.

Pl. 837. J. Horemans the elder: *The poacher denounced* (*s*).
Brussels

Pl. 838. J. Horemans the elder: *Kitchen interior* (*s*).
Dublin N.G.I.

PLATE 839

Pl. 839. P. Snyers: *Market vendors with fruit, fish and ram* (s). Amsterdam Rijks.

Pl. 840. Joseph van Bredael: *Riverside village with gentry and peasants* (s and 1723). Amsterdam Rijks.

Pl. 841. T. Michau: *Riverside village with peasants and cattle* (*doc.*). Madrid

Pl. 842. C. Breydel: *Military movements by a river* (s). Vienna Liecht.

Pl. 843. A. F. Rubens: *Merrymaking outside a tavern* (s). Copenhagen

Pl. 844. A. F. Rubens: *Carnival in Italian landscape* (*s*). Copenhagen

Pl. 845. H. Goovaerts: *Carnival in a palace* (*s* and 1714). Brussels

PLATE 846

Pl. 846. C. van Falens: *Hunters assembling* (*m* and *doc.*). Paris Louvre

Pl. 847. A. de Gryef: *Huntsman and trophies in a landscape* (*s*). Paris Louvre

Pl. 848. J. B. Govaerts: *Game piece with dead boar in a landscape* (*s*). Baltimore (U.S.A.)

PLATE 849

Pl. 849. P. F. de Hamilton: *Wolves and dead hind* (s and 1720). Vienna Kunsthist.

Pl. 850. J. G. de Hamilton: *Horses grazing* (*s*). Vienna Kunsthist.

Pl. 851. P. F. de Hamilton: *Deer and porcupine* (*s* and 1724). Vienna Kunsthist.

PLATE 852

Pl. 852. J. Plasschaert · Still life with skull and engravings (s and 1741/2). Barnard Castle

Pl. 853. H. de La Pegnia : *Paris, Pont Neuf from the Quai de l'Horloge* (*s* and 1743). Vienna Kunsthist.

Pl. 854. H. de La Pegnia : *Paris, Pont Neuf from the Quai de la Mégisserie* (*s*). Vienna Kunsthist.

PLATE 855

Pl. 855. M. J. Geeraerts: *Allegory of Peace* (*s* and 1753). Vienna Liecht.

Pl. 856. P. Snyers: *Landscape with duck pond and children pointing to a bird's nest* (s). Antwerp

Pl. 857. P. Casteels III: *Flowerpiece on a terrace with parrot and monkey* (s). Barnard Castle

PLATE 858

Pl. 858. J. Garemyn: *Building the Ghent Canal* (*doc.*). Bruges

Pl. 859. J. Beerblock: *Procession of the Tailors' Guild in Bruges, Place du Braamberg* (s and 1788). Bruges

Pl. 860. J. Garemyn: *The vegetable market in Bruges* (s and 1778). Bruges

PLATE 861

Pl. 861. J. Horemans the younger: *A landlord and his tenant* (*s* and 1764). New York Met.

PLATE 862

Pl. 862. G. de Spinny: *A lady with a rose* (*s* and 1762). Amsterdam Rijks.

Pl. 863. H. J. Antonissen: *Wooded landscape with figures and cattle* (s and 1787). Cambridge Fitz.

Pl. 864. H. van Lint: *Italian lake with boats and fishermen* (s and 1756). Cambridge Fitz.

Pl. 865. H. van Lint: *Italian landscape with figures and cattle* (s and 1756). Cambridge Fitz.

PLATE 866

Pl. 866. L. B. Coclers: *Catharina Six, Wife of Jan Bicker, seated by a table with trinket box and flowers* (s and 1776).
Amsterdam Rijks

PLATE 867

Pl. 867. W. J. Herreyns: *Adoration of the Magi (doc.)*. Brussels

PLATE 868

Pl. 868. G. de Pélichy: *The Empress Maria Theresa wearing a gown covered with Brussels lace* (*doc*.). Bruges Town Hall

Pl. 870. G. de Pélichy: *The Emperor Joseph II (doc.)*.
Bruges Town Hall

Pl. 869. J. J. Lens: *The Emperor Leopold II (s and 1791)*.
Brussels

PLATE 871

Pl. 871. A. C. Lens: *Ariadne consoled by Bacchus* (*doc.*). Brussels

Pl. 872. P. J. Verhaghen: *S. Stephen receiving the Pope's ambassadors* (s and 1770). Vienna Kunsthist.

Pl. 873. P. J. Verhaghen: *The dismissal of Hagar* (s and 1781). Antwerp

PLATE 874

Pl. 874. L. Defrance: *Portrait of a member of the Jalheau family* (s and 1768). Brussels

PLATE 875

Pl 875. J. L. Demarne: *A country road* (*doc.* 1814) (detail). Paris Louvre

Pl. 876. B. P. Ommeganck: *Landscape with cattle, goats and sheep* (s and 1781). Paris Louvre

Pl. 877. J. F. Legillon: *A stable in Switzerland* (s and 1780). Bruges

PLATE 878

Pl. 878. P. de Glimes: *A young man in a hat* (*s* and 1793). Cambridge Fitz.

Pl. 879. L. Defrance: *The rope dancer* (*s*). New York Met.

Pl. 880. L. Defrance: *Detail of Pl. 879*

PLATE 881

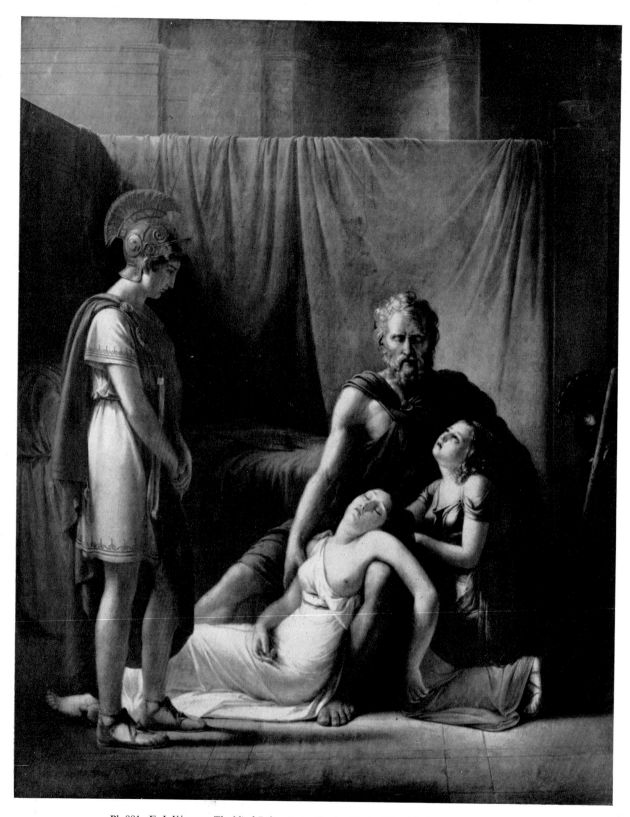

Pl. 881. F. J. Kinson: *The blind Belisarius at the deathbed of his wife Antonina* (s). Bruges

Pl. 882. J. D. Odevaere: *Self portrait with F. J. Wynckelman, President of Bruges Academy Council and the Director J. van der Donckt* (s and 1805). Bruges

Pl. 883. J. B. Suvée: *The daughter of Butades drawing the shadow of her lover* (doc. 1799). Bruges

Pl. 885. F. J. Kinson: *Portrait of a lady (doc.).* Barnard Castle

Pl. 884. F. J. Kinson: *Laetitia Bonaparte (Mme. Mère) (doc.).*
Barnard Castle

PLATE 886

Pl. 886. J. F. van Dael: *Flowers and fruit* (*s* and 1810). Paris Louvre

Pl. 888. J. Eliaerts: *Flowers* (s). Antwerp

Pl. 887. P. Faes: *Flowers and fruit* (s and 1794). Bruges

PLATE 889

Pl. 889. J. van der Donckt: *Sylvie de la Rue and her dog* (*doc.*). Bruges

PLATE 890

Pl. 890. F. J. Navez: *The Hemptinne family* (*doc.* 1816). Brussels

PLATE 891

Pl. 891. P. van Hanselaere: *Susanna and the Elders* (*s* and 1820). Amsterdam Rijks.

PLATE 892

Pl. 892. J. B. de Jonghe: *Market day in Courtrai* (*s* and 1828). Amsterdam Rijks.

Pl. 893. F. de Braekeleer: *Antwerp citadel after the bombardment 1832* (*s*). Amsterdam Rijks.

Pl. 894. J. L. Demarne: *Fair in front of an inn* (*doc.* 1814). Paris Louvre

Pl. 895. E. J. Verboeckhoven: *Boy and cattle in a field* (s and 1824). Amsterdam Rijks.

Pl. 896. A. C. M. Engel: *Wooded landscape with cattle* (s and 1827). Amsterdam Rijks.